BANGLADESH

Frontispiece   Jute-loaded country boats
and the sidewheeler 'Rocket' steamer that
plies to Khulna, on the Burhiganga at
Dacca.

BANGLADESH

by

B. L. C. JOHNSON

Professor of Geography
Australian National University

HEINEMANN EDUCATIONAL BOOKS

LONDON

BARNES & NOBLE BOOKS

NEW YORK

(a division of Harper & Row Publishers Inc)

Published by Heinemann Educational Books Ltd.
48 Charles Street, London W1X 8AH

ISBN 0 435 35486 8

Published in the U.S.A. 1975 by
Harper & Row Publishers Inc
Barnes & Noble Import Division
ISBN 0-06-493343-1

Filmset in Photon Times 11 on 12 pt. by
Richard Clay (The Chaucer Press), Ltd., Bungay, Suffolk
and printed in Great Britain by
Fletcher & Son, Ltd., Norwich

CONTENTS

1. Bangladesh – Political Antecedents   1

2. Landforms   8

3. Climate   15

4. Natural Hazards   23

5. Traditional Agriculture   29

6. Agricultural Regions   48

7. Agricultural Change   56

8. Population and Cities   73

9. Industry and Communications   85

10. Development Prospects   95

    Bibliographical Note   97

    General Index   99

    Index to Places   103

To my new-found land

PREFACE

Born out of bloodshed in 1971 Bangladesh is the achievement of self-determination by the Bangalee nation. This study reviews briefly the historical background of the country's political geography: how in hope it sought partition from the British Indian Empire in 1947 as the eastern wing of Pakistan, but found its political aspirations frustrated and its economic development retarded by successive administrations unable and often seemingly unwilling to plan for equality of opportunity between East and West; and how ultimately the geography of separation, physical and cultural, produced inevitably a second tragic dismemberment.

Economic development over this period is examined in the context of the country's difficult environment of seasonally alternating flood and drought, and occasional devastating cyclone. Food production has lagged behind population growth, and the prospects for increasing output by applying the technology of the 'green revolution' are considered. Eventually fewer people will be able to grow the food required and the need will increase for jobs to be created in urban industry. The resource base and present state of industrialisation, and its demographic influence on urbanisation is assessed.

B. L. C. J.

Canberra
August, 1974

ACKNOWLEDGEMENTS

Many people have by their help contributed to making this book possible. In naming a few I hope that those whose assistance has gone unmentioned will forgive me.

I am indebted to Bangladesh's first High Commissioner in Canberra, Mr. Hossain Ali, and to his staff, particularly Mr Zia Choudhury; to his successor as High Commissioner, Mr. S. A. M. S. Khibria; to Mr. A. W. Shams-ul Alam, Director-General in the Foreign Office, Dacca, who smoothed my paths through officialdom; to Mr. J. L. Allen, first Australian High Commissioner in Dacca and 'first friend' of Bangladesh, and to his successor, Mr. Phillip Flood, both of whom kindly read the text in preparation and made valuable comments; to Mr. S. V. Allison, I.R.B.D. Dacca; to Dr. Aziz-ul-Haq and Mr. Mahboob Alam of the Rural Academy, Comilla; to Mr. A. Z. M. Obaidullah Khan, Department of Rural Development and Co-operatives; to Mr. M. A. Hakim, Deputy Director of Agricultural Statistics, and his assistants who helped me in Shed 29; to my old friend Dr. Aminul Islam, Head of the Department of Geography at the University of Dacca, who gave me academic sanctuary, and with his colleagues a warm welcome back; and last but by no means least to Dr. Mazharul Huq, who periodically over seventeen years has sympathetically answered my questions and tutored me in Bangalee ways.

I am grateful to Oxford University Press for permission to quote from *Disaster in Bangladesh*, edited by Lincoln C. Chew, and to Macmillian Publishers, Ltd. for the selections from *Glimpses of Bengal* by Rabindranath Tagore.

Closer to home I am grateful to those who have deciphered my scribblings to type the manuscript, to Mrs. Pam Millwood for her creative skill with the maps, and to my research assistants Mrs. Bellamy, Mrs. Quiggin and Mr. Andrew Turner. As always, my wife has borne the brunt of my neglect of domestic chores. I thank her also for reading the text with a critical eye, and my daughter Nina for assisting with the distribution maps.

FIGURES

Numbering of figures is by chapter and section

1.1	Districts and towns by size classes	2
1.2	(a) Muslims 1941 as percentage of total population	5
	(b) Muslims 1961 as percentage of total population	5
2.1	Rivers	9
2.2	Geological formations and generalised physiographic types	11
3.1	Percentage of possible sunshine received each month.	17
3.2	Rainfall: monthly dispersion diagrams and annual isohyets	19
3.3	Seasonal rainfall:	
	(a) dry season	20
	(b) *chota barsat*	20
	(c) rainy season	20
3.4	October rainfall:	
	(a) average	22
	(b) 1935	22
4.1	(a) Cyclone trajectories in the Bay of Bengal	23
	(b) Cyclone mortality	24
4.2	River régimes	27
4.3	Floods, their extent and depth	28
5.1	Level of food grain self-sufficiency by districts	31
5.2	Cropping calendar	33
5.3	Aus: percentage of total cropped area	38
5.4	Jute: percentage of total cropped area	40
5.5	Bhadoi crops compared with aman	40
5.6	Transplanted aman: percentage of total cropped area	41
5.7	Broadcast aman: percentage of total cropped area	42
5.8	Dry rabi crops: percentage of total cropped area	43
5.9	Pulses	
	(a) 1944–45	44
	(b) 1969–70	44
5.10	Oilseeds	
	(a) 1944–45	44
	(b) 1969–70	44
5.11	Wheat	
	(a) 1944–45	45
	(b) 1969–70	45
5.12	Sugar Cane and Mills	
	(a) 1944–45	45
	(b) 1969–70	45
5.13	Boro: see also Fig. 7.5	46
6.1	Rice crop combinations	48
6.2	Agricultural regions	48
6.3	Chittagong Hill Tracts showing the main areas and types of lowland cultivation	50
6.4	Malangipara: a typical village of shifting and permanent cultivators	54
7.1	Rice: total area and production, 1947–71	57
7.2	Rice: area and production by types	57
7.3	Rice: yields by types	58
7.4	Cultivation calendar: High Yielding Varieties	61–62
7.5	Boro: areas under traditional and H.Y. Varieties by districts	63
7.6	Tubewells and low lift pumps by districts	64
7.7	Ganges–Kobadak Scheme Phase I	64
7.8	Tubewell layout	68
7.9	Brahmaputra Right Bank Embankment Project	69
7.10	Dacca–Demra Project	70
7.11	Patharghata Coastal Embankment	71

8.1 Population 1961   74
8.2 Population change 1951–61, by thanas   75
8.3 Rural population density per unit of
      cropped area, 1970 estimates   75
8.4 Cropping intensity 1944–45, by sub-
      divisions (except Sylhet District)   76
8.5 Cropping intensity 1960, by sub-
      divisions   76

8.6 Age–sex pyramids for total, urban and
      rural population, 1961   78
8.7 Masculinity in age group 20–39   79
8.8 Dacca and Narayanganj   81
8.9 Chittagong   84
9.1 River communications open all year   90
9.2 Roads and Railways   92

TABLES

Numbering of tables is by chapter and section

3.1 Average monthly maximum and minimum temperature   17
3.2 Rainfall by seasons   18
3.3 Monthly rainfall medians   21
3.4 Monthly rainfall variability   22
5.1 Food intake: grams per person per day   31
7.1 Average yields of rice   58
7.2 Area of crops, Kushtia, Phase I   65
7.3 Crop areas Thakurgaon Tubewell Project   66
7.4 Crop areas Dacca–Demra Scheme   68

PHOTOGRAPHS

Frontispiece Jute-loaded country boats and the sidewheeler 'Rocket' steamer at Dacca   ii

1 Old Mosque at Sylhet   2
2 Modern Mosque at Dacca and cycle rickshaws   3
3 Hindu shrines at Chaggalnaya beside a tank   4
4 Buddhist Kyaung (village temple) near Rangamati   4
5 River Meghna in flood   10
6 A yam leaf serves as umbrella for this farmer in Panchbibi   15
7 Grain silo near Narayanganj, for storing imported foodstuffs   29
8 Street market – vegetables and spices   30
9 Net fishing on a tank near Dacca   30
10 Bangalee homestead   32
11 Gumti River, Comilla   34
12 Ploughing on the Demra Scheme   34
13 Threshing paddy: muzzled cattle treading out the crop, Cox's Bazar   34
14 Threshing by hand, Kushtia District   35
15 Pulling and bundling paddy seedlings for the transplanted *boro* crop at Demra   36
16 Harvesting *aman* paddy at Demra   36
17 Raising water by bucket swinging   37
18 Traditional water scoop or *dunga* used to raise water up to 0·5 metres   38
19 Cutting jute   39
20 Ox- and buffalo-drawn carts bringing sugar cane   46
21 Tipra woman weaving a skirt length on the verandah of her home in the Chittagong Hill Tracts   51
22 Tenchaungya tribal house built on piles, near Rangamati, Chittagong Hill Tracts   51

23 Recently abandoned jhum clearing with temporary hut in Chittagong Hill Tracts   51
24 Magh houses and Chief's local transport, Chittagong Hill Tracts   52
25 Elephant working teak logs. Chittagong Hill Tracts, near Chandraghona   52
26 Jhum and Valley paddy: Chittagong Hill Tracts   52
27 Kaptai Lake, near the hydroelectric station   53
28 Magh houses at Bandarban, Chittagong Hill Tracts: pigs and poultry scavenge beneath the buildings   53
29 Mro houses, Chittagong Hill Tracts: this tribe depends entirely on shifting cultivation   53
30 Mro woman and child ginning cotton on the verandah of their bamboo home in Chittagong Hill Tracts   55
31 Pruning tea bushes, Sylhet District   55
32 'Ammunition' for the green revolution – sacks of potash and superphosphate fertiliser on the Karnaphuli bank   59
33 Low lift pump irrigating transplanted paddy   62
34 Ganges–Kobadak Project pump houses lifting water into Kushtia canal   65
35 Drilling a tubewell near Feni, Noakhali District   67
36 Lined channel of tubewell irrigation project, Thakurgaon, Dinajpur District   67
37 Pump house at Demra   70
38 Agricultural labourers' home: 2 metres square, 1·5 m high   72

39 Palanquin carrying a Muslim lady
       observing purdah   74
40 Downtown Dacca: Motijheel Com-
       mercial area's modern buildings   80
41 Moghul period brick building, Lalbagh,
       Dacca   80
42 Street market – buttons, pens, spoons   82
43 Dacca Sadarghat waterfront: 'bustee'
       shelters along foreshore: country
       boats and ferry steamer   82
44 Workers' housing at a large jute mill
       near Dacca   83
45 Sylhet No. 2 gas exploration well   86
46 Jute press, Narayanganj, for reducing
       the volume of jute bales for export   87
47 Unloading loose skeins of jute   87
48 Jute mill – weaving gunny for sacking   88
49 Workers' housing at Chandraghona
       Paper Mills   88

50 Jute mill near Narayanganj, showing
       the bungalows of supervisory staff in
       the foreground   89
51 Stacks of raw jute at a Chittagong mill   89
52 Bidi making, Bheramara Kushtia
       District   89
53 Raft of bamboo poles with huts on deck
       – Karnaphuli River   91
54 King George VI Bridge at Bhairab
       Bazar: part destroyed during the
       struggle for independence, but now
       repaired   93
55 Overcrowded transport is the rule –
       country bus coming into Dacca   93
56 Loading jute over side from dumb-
       barge at Chalna anchorage, Mongla
       Port on River Pusur   94
57 Chittagong wharves along right bank of
       Karnaphuli River   94

CHAPTER ONE

BANGLADESH–
POLITICAL ANTECEDENTS

The stresses and strains which in 1971 culminated in the failure and collapse of the political structure that was Pakistan were deepseated and had been long present, firmly woven into the fabric of South Asia. The appearance of a new country, Bangladesh, is in some respects merely the latest episode of a series of nationalistic ferments in the sub-continent. The body politic of the neighbouring Indian Union Republic has been subject to several painful convulsions as the demand for self-determination by linguistic 'nations' has been conceded, with the establishment of States based upon a measure of linguistic homogeneity.

The tragedy of Bangladesh – the two dozen years of relative neglect which left the country at the start of independence probably the poorest nation in the world, not to mention the human sufferings of those who resisted recent oppression or became refugees to India – was that Bangalees were persuaded in the 1940s to seek independence of British rule and at the same time a guarantee of relief from Hindu economic domination, through the idea of a single Muslim nation, Pakistan. Religion rather than language, and all that the latter means for communication between human beings, was the sole basis for Pakistan, and it was, at that, the negative aspects of religion that dominated specifically anti-Hindu prejudices.

Mutual antipathy, antagonism and not infrequently violence have coloured the relations between Muslim and Hindu in South Asia for a thousand years. Muslim invaders from Iran and Afghanistan brought their proselytising religion, Islam, to the northwest of the sub-continent in the tenth century A.D. The invaders soon occupied the Punjab Plains and moving into the Ganges Plains established their capital in Delhi. Under the greatest of the Moghul emperors, Akbar (1542–1605), the

Muslims ruled an empire stretching as far east as Bengal and south well into the Indian Peninsula to the latitude of Bombay.

In the process of establishing their political control over the Ganges Plains the Muslims converted many Bangalees to the Islamic faith, from both Hinduism and Buddhism. They also introduced Urdu, the language of the Delhi court, while Bengali literature continued as the vernacular in this eastern province of the Moghul Empire. With the arrival of the East India Company, Moghul power declined and the commercially more involved and astute Hindu prospered in the new environment. To the poor peasant Muslim tenant the Hindu landlord, merchant and moneylender, often combined in a single person, might well have been a man to fear and resent. It is not surprising therefore that as the prospects grew for self-determination and independence from British rule, the mass of the Muslim people could be persuaded that a complete break from India with its Hindu majority was the only acceptable answer. Two major political parties in undivided India came to represent the mass movement for independence of British rule. The Indian National Congress, formed in 1885, was initially broadly based with many influential Muslim members. While inevitably the Congress Party reflected the aspirations of the Hindu majority in the country, its not insignificant Muslim membership was some guarantee that its policies were not drawn on narrow communal lines. By contrast the Muslim League, founded in 1906 at a meeting held in Dacca, was essentially a political party to protect the communal interests of Indian Muslims from the greater political power of Congress. It was within these two parties that the alternative schemes for structuring an ultimately independent India were argued,

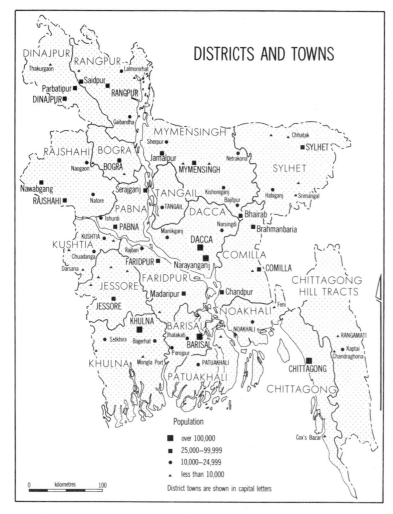

FIG. 1.1   Districts and towns by size classes.

1.   Old mosque at Sylhet.

2. Modern mosque at Dacca with cycle rickshaws in the foreground.

Congress insisting on an All-India federal solution while the League manoeuvred towards separatism.

The idea of an independent Muslim nation in South Asia dates from about 1920, but it is noteworthy that for some twenty years the concept related only to parts or all of what became West Pakistan, together with Kashmir, and left Bengal out of the picture. A more or less Muslim majority province had existed briefly in Assam and East Bengal during the period of the first attempt to partition Bengal on communal lines, an early sign that the British were prepared to alter boundaries in a way that might engender nationalism. This partition however, stimulated a reaction particularly among Hindu Bangalees who felt their cultural nation was being divided irrespective of its religious duality, and who understandably felt their political and economic power, exerted from Calcutta, to be seriously threatened. For a few years, from 1905 to 1912, Dacca was a provincial capital, and some of the city's finest buildings date from that period.

In 1930, however, when the poet–philosopher Muhammad Iqbal addressed the Muslim League he spoke of a possible Muslim state comprising the Punjab, Northwest Frontier Province and Baluchistan; Sind, a portion of the then Bombay Presidency, and the Indian princely state of Kashmir were left out, as was any reference to Bengal with its very large Muslim population. Chaudhuri Rahmat Ali, who in 1933 coined the name Pakistan for the proposed Muslim state, neglected to fit Bengal into his scheme or into his imperfect acronym: P for Punjab, A for Afghania (N.W. Frontier Province), K for Kashmir, S for Sind, Tan for Baluchistan. The Pakistan National Movement, of which Rahmat Ali was founder-president, did not entirely disregard Bengal but rather urged that it should have a separate national movement, as also the Nizam of Hyderabad's 'Dominions'.

El Hamza, writing in 1941, propounded the case for an independent northwestern state of Pakistan, pointing out the great differences between it and the Muslim majority region of Bengal, about whose national self-determination he did not feel competent to comment.

The Muslim League in 1940 proclaimed a policy to demand *two* independent Muslim states, a northwestern and a northeastern, but in the subsequent political developments Jinnah apparently saw the possibility of achieving a single Muslim Pakistan state when partition of All-India became inevitable. The drive for this solution came from the Punjabi core of the Pakistan movement. Bangalees were not fully convinced, even as late as 1947, when a proposal for an undivided independent Bengal was mooted.

The act of partition in 1947 established the frontiers of what is now Bangladesh. The greater part of the old Province of Bengal together with most of the Sylhet District lying in the adjacent continuation of the delta plain into Assam to the northeast, became East Bengal, later called East Pakistan. In most of the area there was a clear Muslim majority, excepting Khulna (49·3 per cent) and Chittagong Hill Tracts (2·8 per cent Muslim) (Fig. 1.2a). Murshidabad (56·6 per cent Muslim) went to India as did Hindu majority portions of four districts near the border with West Bengal. In the case of the Chittagong Hill Tracts the semi-tribal population

3. Hindu shrines at Chaggalnaya near Feni, beside a tank.

was predominantly Buddhist, and the area could hardly be administered effectively except through Chittagong.

Partition cut off Calcutta (23 per cent Muslim) from an important part of its economic hinterland, and when political relations became bad East Bengal was denied access to its traditional markets for raw jute. The population of the new East Bengal included almost 29 per cent Hindus, while 25 per cent of West Bengal's population was Muslim. It is some measure of the strength of the common Bangalee cultural inheritance that partitioned Bengal saw relatively much less of the traumatic uprooting of refugees on either side that marked the partition of the Punjab. Refugee movements there were, but they mostly came later, some of them, it is claimed, by writers like J. K. Ray, at the instigation of West Pakistani inspired *agents provocateurs*.

The maps in Fig. 1.2 show the percentage of Muslims by districts in undivided Bengal (with Sylhet District of Assam) in 1941, and in East Pakistan in 1961. It is clear that there was still a substantial minority of non-Muslims in 1961 totalling almost 10 million, and there is no reason to suppose a radical change in the pattern of distribution of this minority in present-day Bangladesh. However, between 1941 and 1961 the proportion of Muslims everywhere increased, though it is not possible to make precise comparisons for the districts that changed their boundaries as a result of partition. The largest minorities in 1961 proportionately to the Muslim population were in the Chittagong Hill Tracts where non-Muslim tribal groups made up 88 per cent of the population in 1961 and in the western border districts of Dinajpur (31·4 per cent), Khulna (39·8 per cent) and Jessore

4. Buddhist kyaung (village temple), near Rangamati. Built of bamboo on timber piles, thatched with sunn grass, a notched trunk as staircase.

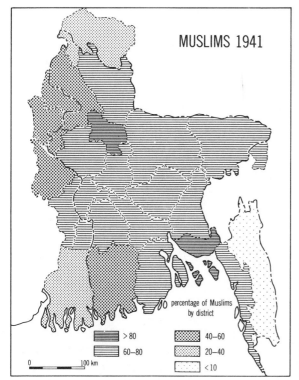

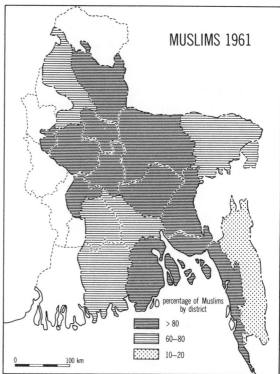

FIG. 1.2 (*a*)   Percentage of Muslims by districts 1941. The full area of districts partitioned between West Bengal (India) and East Bengal (Pakistan) in 1947 is shown with the final boundary superimposed.

FIG. 1.2 (*b*)   Percentage of Muslims by districts, 1961.

(28·2 per cent). Faridpur (26·2 per cent) has a substantial number of scheduled caste Hindus, and Sylhet (26·9 per cent) is the home of most of the Hindu workers on tea plantations.

Mention must be made of the Biharis, who although not a minority group in the religious sense, find themselves, as Urdu speakers, a linguistic minority in a land of Bangalees. At the time of partition many thousands of Muslim Biharis migrated, along with Muslim Bangalees, from India to what is now Bangladesh. They now number perhaps 400,000 and represent Bangladesh's largest minority problem. In that many of them were understandably sympathetic to West Pakistani interests on account of their linguistic affinity, the whole group has been under a cloud of suspicion since the declaration of Bangalee independence in 1971 and through the civil war that followed.

From the start, the disunity within Pakistan was apparent. Religion proved inadequate to hold different peoples together in amity. The West Pakistani tended to look down on the Bangalee as a 'second class Muslim', descendant of converts, and so not in the same direct line of religious purity as those who could look back to ancestors who brought Islam to the country. Furthermore the West Pakistanis, more specifically the Punjabi Muslims, could see themselves as direct heirs to the ruling tradition of the Moghul Empire in which of course Bengal had been a subjugated territory. Under the British, Punjabis formed the élite fighting troops of the Indian Army while Bangalees were regarded as a non-martial people suitable at best for employment in the military as clerks.

Thus there were deep-seated cultural prejudices current at the birth of Pakistan. The Bangalees were perhaps innately more provincial in outlook, justly proud of a rich linguistic heritage which had been strengthened by developments in Bengali literature under the stimulus of British education in the nineteenth century. They were democratic in politics, resentful of oppression from landlord or government,

and without any tradition of militant nationalism. To a considerable extent the Muslim Bangalee
of East Bengal (East Pakistan) maintained loyalty to
a wider Bangalee cultural nationalism that tran-
scended the religious differences between Hindu and
Muslim. At the village level there was much inter-
weaving of the cultural strands and, usually, mutual
respect for religious observances of others. This was
certainly not the case in West Pakistan, where the
Muslims held to a more clearly separatist way of life.
It seems that the Punjabi leaders in the new Pakistan
added to their list of prejudices a strong reservation
about the basic loyalty of the Bangalee.

The Bangalee's sense of democracy and pride in
his culture was soon affronted by the manifestation
of West Pakistani attitudes which may be summed
up in a determination not to allow the greater numbers of the population of East Pakistan ever to
achieve political domination in the Pakistan state
and to counter any tendency to secede. As J. K.
Ray puts it: 'Since the emergence of Pakistan as an
independent state, those who dominated the Central
Government, remaining predominantly West
Pakistani in composition . . . have consistently tried
to impose (and greatly succeeded too) a cultural,
economic and political hegemony* upon East
Pakistan.'

The realities of the situation became evident
when within a year of independence Punjabis
promoted a policy to proclaim Urdu alone as the
national language of Pakistan, and even to substitute Urdu's Arabic script for the Nagari script in
Bengali. While Urdu is the mother tongue of only a
minority in West Pakistan it serves there as an
acceptable *lingua franca*. In East Bengal the urban
population speaks Urdu to a small extent, but the
regional language is undoubtedly Bengali. As to
scripts, Urdu is written in a script derived from
Arabic which is the language and script of the
Muslim's holy book the Koran. Those who wanted
to impose on East Bengal an Arabicised Bengali
thought thereby to drive a wedge between Muslim
and Hindu in Bengal and so to reduce the risks of
secession.

The intention to make Urdu the single national
language of Pakistan was announced by Jinnah, the
acknowledged father of the Pakistan state and its

* Hegemony: predominance of one state in a confederacy:
OED.

governor-general, during a visit to Dacca in 1948,
eight months after the achievement of independence. There followed immediate hostile reaction to
the proposals, and the man who was subsequently
to become the architect and founder of Bangladesh,
Sheikh Mujibur Rahman, was arrested in a demonstration about the language issue at that time.
Protests continued over the next four years despite
vigorous police repression, and ultimately Bengali
was accepted as a national language on an equal
footing with Urdu.

However, although the Bangalees showed they
could not be bullied into submission on cultural
matters, they were to remain politically under-
privileged and economically subservient in
undivided Pakistan. The constitution was engin-
eered to ensure that the East wing could not use its
demographic superiority in numbers to gain
political ascendancy over the peoples of West
Pakistan. The internal political history of Pakistan
is punctuated by the repeated demands for autonomy for East Pakistan, as repeatedly resisted by the
Central Government. It is hard to avoid the conclusion that politically and economically the
government, dominated by West Pakistanis, planned
and systematically imposed a form of 'colonialism'
on the East.

Bangalees claim that discrimination was widespread against them in the armed services, in technical and higher education generally, and in the
public service. The discrimination came about
mainly through gross inequalities of opportunity
between the two wings.

It was however in the economic sphere that the
evidence for the West's domination of the East was
most clear. The political weakness of the East during the years when there was some form of democratic government and even more so through the
periods of quasi-military dictatorship, prevented
effective opposition to the Central Government's
policies. Two examples will demonstrate the
processes of economic exploitation.

Jute was the mainstay of the Pakistan economy.
It was produced wholly in the East wing and exported either raw or manufactured to overseas markets. Yet the foreign exchange earned from jute had
to pass directly to the Centre where the decisions
were taken as to how the money would be allocated.
The revenues from taxes and tariffs were collected

by the Central Government and disbursed very unequally. In 1956 it was estimated that East Pakistan received Rupees $1\frac{1}{8}$ per head from Central revenues while the West had Rupees 32.

Industrial development was largely in the hands of West Pakistanis, and the East became a large protected market for their products. East Pakistan bought much more from the West than it sold to the West and had in a sense to find the balance from exports, economically a typical 'colonial' situation.

That it was easier to develop West Pakistan, and probably impossible to ensure an even spread of economic advance in both wings brought little comfort to the Bangalees who felt they would be better off on their own. The standard of living of the West Pakistani was estimated to be 60 per cent higher than that of the Bangalee, and the reasons are not hard to find. Investment by Central Government in the first capital, Karachi, and later in a new capital at Islamabad near Rawalpindi, in the many training institutions in the West (which had minimal counterparts in the more populous East), in the remodelling of the irrigation system of the West, with the help of vast sums from the World Bank, all went to increase the job opportunities in the West, to put more money into circulation there and so to raise the standards of living and the people's sense of progress. Scarcely any of this economic development benefited East Pakistan where investment lagged, where the economic infrastructure was weaker and where a naturally difficult environment was periodically smitten by catastrophic floods and cyclones.

Despite the absence of truly democratic government in Pakistan the pressures for East Bengal autonomy grew, and the Central Government began belatedly to plan for a more equitable distribution of resources for development. After years of dictatorship and the experiment with 'basic democracy' which denied the public a direct vote except at the local government level, general elections on the basis of universal adult suffrage were held in December 1970. In East Pakistan the result of the elections was a landslide victory for the Awami League led by Sheikh Mujibur Rahman, whose party, by winning 167 seats, gained an absolute majority in the Pakistan National Assembly of 313 seats. Mujibur Rahman's election platform had been his 'six points' including: a federal system of government with the centre responsible only for foreign policy and defence; a separate economic policy for East Pakistan, allowing it to receive its proportionate share of foreign exchange earnings; its own militia, military academy and ordnance factory; the establishment of the Pakistan Naval Headquarters in the East wing.

The fundamental issue from which stemmed the chain of events which produced the civil war and the mass migration of millions of refugees to India, and ultimately India's intervention to force a military settlement, was Mujibur Rahman's demand that his electoral victory entitled his party to confirm in the National Assembly his six points as the basis for the new constitution which had been promised by the President. President Yahya Khan and Mr. Bhutto, leader of the majority party in West Pakistan, refused to accept this claim, saying that the constitution had to be agreed by the governments of each wing and not by a simple majority of the National Assembly. For Sheikh Mujibur Rahman this refusal could be seen as the last straw in a decade of denials of Bangalee self-determination. On 26 March 1971, following the brutal 'crack-down' by the army at midnight on 25/26 March, the independence of Bangladesh was proclaimed and the struggle became a civil war, terminating in victory in December, after the '14-day war', in which Indian military help was a decisive factor.

CHAPTER TWO

LANDFORMS

Traditional agriculture in Bangladesh has over the centuries become adapted to the physical environment so that it varies in detail over the country in response to local and regional differences of geomorphology and hydrology and through the year to the incidence of rainfall. Plans for agricultural development in the future must also take account of the basic physical conditions, some of which may be modified by the application of modern technology, but many aspects of which have still to be accepted as largely immutable and to which the cultivator must still adapt his practices however sophisticated they may have become in a scientific sense.

GEOMORPHOLOGY

An understanding of the landforms of the country – its geomorphology – is essential to any appreciation of its agricultural problems. Water is the fundamental factor in Bangalee agriculture whether it be direct rainfall, the floodwaters of rivers or ground water held in aquifers below the surface. The agricultural practices and potential of an area are greatly influenced by the lie of the land, whether it floods deeply or for long periods, whether its soils retain moisture in droughty times, and how high above and distant from sources of surface or underground water the fields may be in the dry season.

The Hill Country
More than 90 per cent of the total area of Bangladesh is lowland, the alluvial gift of the several great river systems that traverse the country to reach the Bay of Bengal. Apart from a few Tertiary–Pleistocene outcrops at the foot of the Shillong (Meghalaya) Plateau, including the country's only exposed limestone, of

Eocene age, it is only in the east and southeast, in the districts of Chittagong and the Chittagong Hill Tracts, and to a minor extent in Sylhet, that the seemingly monotonous alluvial plains give way to steeply dissected hill country. Here the roughly north–south trend of the parallel ridges of sedimentary rocks of Miocene, Pliocene and Pleistocene age is picked out clearly in the pattern of subsequent drainage. The formations are mainly sandstones, sandy clays, shales and siltstones. A few major rivers traverse the ridges, notably the Karnaphuli, which rises in Assam and flows southwest across the grain of the country to enter the Bay of Bengal at Chittagong whose port makes use of the river's estuary. The Feni, Sangu and Matamuhari rivers have shorter courses across the hills. All these rivers follow more or less lengthy north–south sections. They represent Bangladesh's only controllable hydroelectric potential, but so far only the Karnaphuli has been harnessed by the construction of an earth dam at Kaptai behind which an extensive lake has been ponded back (Fig. 2.1). The gradient of the hill country rivers is generally slight, though the valley sides rise steeply from narrow, often discontinuous flood plains to ridge crests more than a thousand feet above the valley floor. The highest peak in Bangladesh stands at 1003 m (3292 ft) on the Burma border.

Northwards the ranges of the Chittagong Hills extend into the Indian territory of Tripura from which their counterparts project into the Sylhet Plain. The ridges here generally lie 60–90 m (200–300 ft) above sea level.

In the Chittagong Hill Tracts the bamboo jungle that clothes many slopes is periodically cleared for *jhum* cultivation (shifting agriculture) while the narrow alluvial strips of the longitudinal valley flood

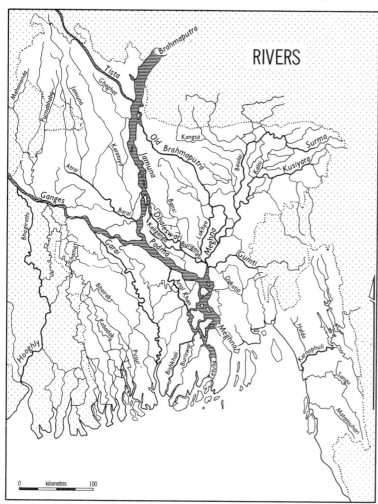

FIG. 2.1 Rivers.

plains support permanent fields. The use of the rivers for power development obviously conflicts with the agricultural economy of the hill tribes, a problem that will be discussed further below.

Fringing the hill country in Sylhet and Chittagong there is often a low benchland up to about 30 m (100 ft) above the neighbouring plain, carrying a red, lateritic, leached silty clay–loam soil similar to that on the old alluvial terraces. These benchlands, because of their relatively good drainage and level surfaces, have attracted development as sites for tea gardens and, in Cox's Bazar Subdivision (south Chittagong), for teak and experimental rubber plantations. The Geological Map of Pakistan (1964) shows the benchlands in part as Pliocene and Pleistocene sedimentary material, and in part under the general category of 'piedmont de-posits', undistinguished from the extensive alluvial fan material of North Bengal, and the alluvial plains of Chittagong. (Fig. 2.2.) It is to be hoped that geomorphological research will clarify the genesis and relationships of these morphological units.

The Plains

Throughout Pleistocene time and up to the present, great rivers have been pouring their sediments into the Bay of Bengal to build up alluvial plains. However, conditions have not remained stable throughout this time. Sea level has not remained constant. At the period of maximum glaciation when there was a world-wide fall in sea level, the coastline may have stood 135 m (c. 440 ft) lower than at present. In adjusting to this low sea level the rivers cut deeply into the deltaic plains they had earlier constructed.

5. River Meghna near its confluence with the Padma (Ganges). This view, taken in August with the river in flood, shows waterlogged fields of paddy and jute. The dark linear features are settlements, built on river levees, their houses hidden beneath trees. The numerous village sites of this kind are an indication of the changeable course of the river.

During warm interglacial periods sea level may have been 30 m (c. 100 ft) higher than now. It is possible that the surfaces of the old alluvial terraces of the Barind, the Madhupur Tract and the fringing benchlands of Sylhet and Chittagong, are related to such a higher sea level. Tectonic instability has also played a part in modelling the landscape. The old alluvial terraces have been deformed by faulting and tilting, and as recently as 1897 earthquake movements caused changes in the course of the Tista. In Mymensingh and Sylhet the Meghna Depression, containing many low-lying permanent lakes or *haors*, is probably due in part to tectonic subsidence.

Two main types of constructional activity are currently at work in the plains. In the northeast the River Tista continues to build up a sandy alluvial fan in large part demarcated as piedmont deposits on the map of geological formations and physiographical types (Fig. 2.2) which has its apex where the river debouches from the Himalaya. Evidence of former courses occupied by the Tista is seen in the 'underfit' channels of the Karatoya, Western Jamuna, Atrai and Purnabhaba (Fig. 2.1). A major upset to the course of the Tista occurred in 1787 when apparently an exceptional flood blocked the Atrai channel, then being used by the Tista, forcing the flow into a course along the present Ghaghat which it occupied until the 1897 earthquake. The sudden influx of Tista water into the Brahmaputra in 1787 may have caused a diversion of the latter into its present north–south channel known as the Jamuna, though tectonic movements in the trough between the Barind and the Madhupur Tract may have been in part responsible.

The North Bengal Sandy Alluvial Fan, until recently a region of only moderate to poor agricultural productivity, has become revitalised by the development of the groundwater resources contained in its coarse sediments. The remainder of the Bangalee lowlands are the realm of the Ganges, Brahmaputra and Meghna river systems flowing in their deltaic stage. A deltaic river flows on an alluvial ridge of its own making, the highest parts of which are the *levees* immediately adjacent to the river's channel. From the levee crest the land slopes away gently into the lowest areas, the *backswamp depressions*. When in full flood the river overtops its levee. The rate of flow of water away from the main channel diminishes rapidly, and with it, its capacity to carry its load of suspended sand, silt and mud. Consequently the coarsest part of the load is deposited first, hence the building of a levee which is invariably coarser material than will be found in the backswamp area. The load carried by one river may well differ from that of another, and so the range of textures of the alluvial material making up its levee–backswamp association varies. The general principle holds however for every river at every scale within the delta plain. Backswamp depressions are generally areas of clays and fine silt; levees, of sand and coarse silt.

The whole delta plain is made up of these recurring associated elements: backswamp depressions and the levees forming their rims. But not all such features in the present landscape are in a state of active evolution. Deltaic rivers, flowing as they do on alluvial ridges, alter their courses from time to time, so gradually constructing their delta, and the

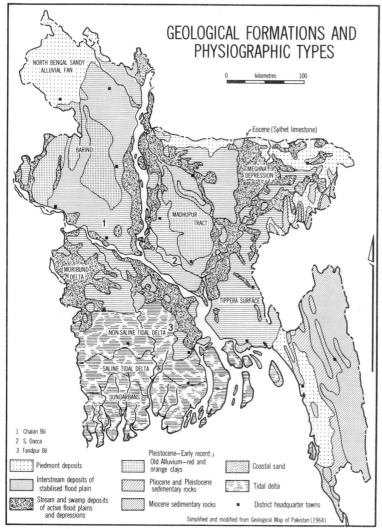

FIG. 2.2 Geological formations and physiographic types.

surface details in any area may be in part the product of a past phase of river action. Similarly the subsurface alluvium may differ from that on the surface due to changes in the location of river channels. The active 'alluvial ridge' of a river will be of sandy material at the surface, but may well be underlain by clay. (It may be noted in passing that river channels cut in clay are relatively stable compared with those excavated in silt or sand.) Beneath the superficial mud and clay of backswamp depressions, sandy layers are generally found indicating the former location of the alluvial ridge. These sand beds are of great importance as rechargeable aquifers from which water may be drawn for dry

season agriculture, to be replenished in the following wet season.

In addition to the fluvial activity discussed above, tidal action should be mentioned as a factor in the formation of the seaward portion of the delta. Its influence will be examined further below.

The dynamic character of the physiography of the delta has been stressed. It is a region of continual change. Some changes are taking place annually, such as the modification in the channels and *char* lands (sand banks) of the major rivers; other changes may be measurable in decades or in centuries, such as the gradual abandoning of its westerly distributaries by the Ganges, whose waters now join with those of the Brahmaputra (which suffers a name change to Jamuna as it enters Bangladesh) to form the Padma till it becomes the Meghna beyond the confluence with that lesser river. The united flow of these rivers finds its way to the sea through a number of distributaries which were becoming progressively more easterly until man-made embankments in Noakhali District arrested the tendency. Now the main flow follows the Shahbazpur and Tetulia Channels, east and west of Bhola Island, and several lesser distributaries, such as the Buriswar and Bishkhali flowing through Patuakhali District.

Time is thus a significant factor in differentiating the various parts of the delta. While in the most active areas channels are constantly changing, in regions long since abandoned by vigorous flood-waters the evidence of former river courses and levee banks is being obliterated by local soil wash.

It is appropriate at this point to sketch out, on the basis of the factors discussed so far, a system of physiographic type-regions in the plains, as a reference base for examining the areal variety of the country's agricultural development problems, many of which are related directly or indirectly to the physical geographical conditions (Fig. 2.2).

The **old alluvial terraces** of the Barind and Madhupur Tract have already been mentioned. The **Barind**, mostly in the districts of Rajshahi and Bogra, is a gently undulating region of heavy impermeable red clay soils. Along the courses of the underfit rivers referred to above there is sandy alluvium, and to the north the clay plain disappears beneath the sandy sediments of the alluvial fan of North Bengal. The intractability of the clays, until thoroughly moistened by monsoon rains, make this area traditionally one of *aman* paddy monoculture. Surface tanks hold water for domestic and stock use. The clay soils, once wet, produce an excellent crop during the rains, but have to rely on direct rainfall since the whole region stands well above the reach of flood waters from the major rivers. Recent investigations have shown the existence here of groundwater resources whose exploitation could substantially alter the local agricultural economy.

Facing the Barind across the Jamuna flood plain, the **Madhupur Tract**, mostly in Dacca District, has a surface more dissected by winding valleys, giving a local relief of 10 m (30 ft) or so. Unlike the Barind, there remains much *sal* (Shorea robusta)

woodland on the rises, and agriculture is largely confined to the valleys.

Next lower in elevation are the more or less *stabilised flood plains* of the major river systems, formed of silt, sand and less commonly fine gravel, termed 'interstream deposits' by the Geological Survey. These are areas over which the rivers may periodically flood, but within which their distributary channels are fairly stable. The stabilised flood plains in Comilla and Noakhali comprise a flat clay lowland standing on average two metres above the adjacent active flood plain of the Meghna to the west. The geologists, Morgan and McIntyre, called this the *Tippera Surface*, and consider that its slightly oxidised soils together with morphological evidence point to the area being a surface of Early Recent geological age. Only on its western flank is the plain regularly inundated by the Meghna, and throughout the area signs of past major river action such as meander traces and levees are lacking. Small though occasionally turbulent rivers like the Gumti cross the plain from the Tripura hill country.

The **North Bengal Alluvial Fan** in Dinajpur and Rangpur Districts is part of the extensive submontane belt of alluvial cones that stretches the length of the Himalayan foothills. Unlike other lowland surfaces in Bangladesh the fan has an appreciable slope of 30 m (*c.* 100 ft) in 80 km (50 miles). In the process of building its fan the River Tista has varied its course from time to time. One of its most westerly channels in the past would have brought its water to the Ganges opposite the latter's distributary into the Mathabanga. The removal of the Tista to join the Jamuna could have contributed to the decay of the Ganges's western distributaries, with serious consequences for the region known as the **Moribund Delta** as far as its agricultural potential is concerned.

Similar genetically to the North Bengal Sandy Alluvial Fan in that they are composed of detrital material from the adjacent hills, but individually of much smaller scale, are a series of piedmont slopes forming an almost continuous belt along the southern base of the Shillong Plateau and the hills of south Sylhet. A separate but comparable zone flanks the hills in Chittagong District.

In Kushtia and Jessore Districts is the Moribund Delta, so called because although the meander belts of former distributaries of the Ganges can be picked out in old levees and in backswamps and swales that fill with water from local drainage in the wet season, the area is no longer inundated by Ganges water. Many of the old channels are blocked with water hyacinth or completely silted up. Watered only by direct rainfall the soils have become leached and badly need the rejuvenation by nutrient-bearing river water which the Ganges–Kobadak irrigation scheme is designed to achieve.

Agriculturally the stabilised flood plain is probably the most productive physiographic element in the country, largely because, except in the Moribund Delta, its fertility is regenerated annually by floodwaters. The broad levees on the left bank of the Ganges–Padma and the right bank of the Old Brahmaputra in Mymensingh are important features within it, as are the isolated 'islands' of interstream deposits that stand above the active flood plains and provide relatively dry and stable sites for district towns like Faridpur and Barisal. Altogether twelve of the country's nineteen district towns are located on the stabilised delta.

The remainder of the low country consists of the active flood plains of the rivers, their backswamps and other depressions, the delta proper or tidal delta with its saline fringe, and some strips of sandy coastal formations.

The great rivers themselves flow in broad braided channels which at low water periods become a series of sandy or silty islands or *chars* completely submerged during the rainy season. The **braided riverain charlands** may be regarded as the **active flood plains** within which the rivers are constantly changing course. The active flood plains are bounded by levees or, at low water, by river cliffs as much as 8 m (*c.* 24 ft) high. In the case of the Brahmaputra–Jumuna the river bed between the cliffs is up to 29 km (18 miles) wide, and that of the Lower Meghna is similar. The sandier banks of the Brahmaputra–Jamuna are a factor in the greater width and instability of its channel compared with that of the Ganges–Padma. However, dramatic course changes occur annually in both rivers, sweeping away villages and creating new charlands.

Several major depressions merit mention: Chalan Bil, a backswamp to the Ganges on its left bank, but also receiving water from the Atrai and Western Jamuna; the Dacca Depression, similarly a Padma left-bank backswamp carrying the Dhaleswari ana-branch; Faridpur Bil, on the right bank of the Padma. Chalan Bil and the Dacca Depression may, in part, be areas of subsidence related to tilting of the Pleistocene terraces of the Barind and Madhupur Tracts respectively, and tectonic movement cannot be discounted as a possible factor explaining the 1800 sq km (700 sq mile) marsh of Faridpur Bil and its westerly extension into Khulna.

Other major depressions form a large part of the country along the base of the Shillong Plateau and in the Meghna basin. Here the cause is almost certainly tectonic and subsidence may be continuing. Some of the lakes are only 3 m (10 ft) above sea level yet almost 320 km (*c.* 200 miles) from the coast. It is not surprising therefore that the Meghna Depression becomes a vast shallow lake for six months or more when the waters discharged into the basin from the surrounding hills are unable to escape southwards through the Meghna because of the higher level of floodwaters in the Old Brahmaputra flowing on its alluvial ridge. All these depressions become extensive water bodies in the rains, and so potential reservoirs for dry season irrigation.

Whereas in the active flood plains the characteristic processes operating are the transport of sediment and the constant remodelling of the channels and charlands, in the tidal delta sedimentation of a more permanent kind becomes more important. Changes continue to occur in the course and the form of the charlands of the most vigorous distributaries, but the majority hold to their channels deep cut below sea level in the deltaic clay. The whole delta proper is tidal to a degree but not all is saline.

The effect of tides is measurable on the flow of the Padma to within 30 km (19 miles) of the confluence of the Ganges and the Brahmaputra–Jamuna, and on the Meghna system well into the heart of the Meghna Depression. Their influence on the geomorphology of the land is appreciable only in what may be termed the **Tidal Delta** where the alternation of tidal and river flow is pronounced, developing in the distributary channels a distinctive elongated hexagonal pattern. The main channels are aligned roughly north to south forming the long axes of the hexagons, which are linked by short east–west sections. Since so close to the sea the sediments are generally very fine, the channels are excavated in clay and tend to be deep and stable.

For example, the Pusur south from Khulna takes ocean-going cargo liners 80 km (50 miles) from its mouth. Tidal scour assists in maintaining deep channels even where fresh water flow in the rivers is minimal. The tides also act to spread the fine sediments more evenly, so that the difference in height between levee and backswamp tends to be less than where river action alone is operative.

The western half of the Tidal Delta is fairly stable morphologically speaking, but from the Tetulia Channel eastwards, where the Lower Meghna's distributaries carry the greater part of discharge of the whole Ganges–Brahmaputra–Meghna system, changes in the distribution of estuarine islands, charlands and water passages are frequent. Man has stepped in to try to control nature to a degree and has succeeded in adding to the mainland area of Noakhali District by diverting the Meghna south into the Shahbazpur Channel and away from its former sweeping course west to east along the coast and to either side of Sandwip Island. However, man interferes with a great river not without some risk, and what has become Noakhali's advantage has been bought at the cost of erosional losses to Hatia and other islands in the estuary.

The periodic hazard of cyclones along the coastal districts of the Bay of Bengal will be examined below. Yet another hazard, and perhaps a more insidious one, is salinity. During the rainy season there is generally enough fresh water on the land from direct rainfall to allow cultivation throughout the cleared areas of the Tidal Delta. In the dry season however, as the fresh water draining from the landward side diminishes, tidal flow enables salt water to penetrate inland. The western Tidal Delta south of the Moribund Delta suffers most in this regard as the channels now carry little or no water from the Ganges, and the alleviation of the serious salinity problem for agriculture in most of Khulna District was one of the long-term objectives of the Ganges–Kobadak scheme. It is no accident of history that the last extensive area of lowland woodland left uncleared by man is in the Khulna Sundarbans, a region of mangroves and swamp forest, the home of tiger, Chital deer and swamp crocodiles. In Barisal and Patuakhali Districts the salinity problem is limited to the coastal strip, since the distributaries east of the Madhumati flow fresh all the year. The area affected by salinity extends north to Pirojpur and Patuakhali and eastwards includes the southern half of Bhola Island and the whole of Hatia and Sandwip. It is anticipated that the salinity problem will spread as more of the dry season flow of the rivers and groundwater sources is utilised for cropping. It is being met in part by the construction of coastal embankments with sluices to control tidal flow.

The plains of Chittagong District repeat on a small scale some of the conditions in the Tidal Delta. The rivers are distinctly tidal, and salinity is a problem for dry season cropping on the lowest parts of the coastal and riverain plains. From the Karnaphuli mouth south to Cox's Bazar a considerable length of coast is protected from tidal saline incursions by embankments. At Cox's Bazar starts a fine sand beach backed by dunes, which extend to the southernmost extremity of mainland Bangladesh in the Naaf Peninsula.

CHAPTER THREE

CLIMATE

The rains of the summer monsoon dominate the seasons in Bangladesh. Statistics cannot adequately convey what the rainy season is like in the delta. The following extracts from the pen of Bengal's most celebrated master of poetry and prose, Rabindranath Tagore, although written sixty years ago, are vividly evocative of the region's climate. They are taken from *Glimpses of Bengal*, being selections from Tagore's letters, published by Macmillan and Co.:

6.   A yam leaf serves as umbrella for this farmer in Panchbibi.

3rd July 1893.

All last night the wind howled like a stray dog, and the rain still pours on without a break. The water from the fields is rushing in numberless, purling streams to the river. The dripping ryots are crossing the river in the ferry-boat, some with their tokas on [conical hats of straw or of split bamboo], others with yam leaves held over their heads. Big cargo-boats are gliding along, the boatman sitting drenched at his helm, the crew straining at the tow-ropes through the rain. The birds remain gloomily confined to their nests, but the sons of men fare forth, for in spite of the weather the world's work must go on.

4th July 1893.

A little gleam of sunlight shows this morning. There was a break in the rains yesterday, but the clouds are banked up so heavily along the skirts of the sky that there is not much hope of the break lasting. It looks as if a heavy carpet of cloud had been rolled up to one side, and at any moment a fussy breeze may come along and spread it over the whole place again, covering every trace of blue sky and golden sunshine.

What a store of water must have been laid up in the sky this year. The river has already risen over the low *chur*-lands [sandbanks], threatening to overwhelm all the standing crops. The wretched ryots, in despair, are cutting and bringing away in boats sheaves of half-ripe rice. As they pass my boat I hear them bewailing their fate. It is easy to understand how heart-rending it must be for cultivators to have to cut down their rice on the very eve of its ripening, the only hope left them being that some of the ears may possibly have hardened into grain.

20th September 1894.

Big trees are standing in the flood water, their trunks wholly submerged, their branches and foliage bending over the waters. Boats are tied up under shady groves of mango and bo tree, and people bathe screened behind them. Here and there cottages stand out in the current, their inner quadrangles under water.

As my boat rustles its way through standing crops it now and then comes across what was a pool and is still to be distinguished by its clusters of water-lilies, and diver-birds pursuing fish.

The water has penetrated every possible place. I have never before seen such a complete defeat of the land. A little more and the water will be right inside the cottages, and their occupants will have to put up *machans* to live on. The cows will die if they have to remain standing like this in water up to their knees. All the snakes have been flooded out of their holes, and they, with sundry other homeless reptiles and insects, will have to chum with man and take refuge on the thatch of his roof.

The vegetation rotting in the water, refuse of all kinds floating about, naked children with shrivelled limbs and enlarged spleens splashing everywhere, the long-suffering patient housewives exposed in their wet clothes to wind and rain, wading through their daily tasks with tucked-up skirts and over all a thick pall of mosquitoes hovering in the noxious atmosphere – the sight is hardly pleasing!

TEMPERATURE

Rainfall is by far the most important climatic element in Bangladesh as far as agriculture is concerned. It is doubtful if day temperatures are ever low enough to arrest plant growth, though in winter the microclimate of flooded paddy-fields is cool enough to delay the maturing of some high yielding varieties of rice recently introduced.

The seasonal march of average monthly maximum and minimum temperatures at Dinajpur and Chittagong are given below. The two stations, despite their differing locations, the first 400 km (250 miles) inland, the second almost on the coast of the Bay of Bengal, have very similar temperature régimes. Temperatures are highest in April when Chittagong's absolute maximum of about 38 °C occurred. Its absolute minimum of 7 °C was in January. Dinajpur's absolute minimum probably approaches freezing point: 3·8 °C has been recorded there and in nearby Jalpaiguri just outside the Bangladesh border, rare frost has been known to damage tobacco crops.

The relatively small annual range of temperature, 10 °C at Dinajpur, 6 °C at Chittagong, is an inadequate measure of the seasonal difference in 'sensible climate' as experienced by man.

The cool dry season, with its clear skies, is extremely pleasant (for those with a house in which to shelter at night). Relative humidity averages 70 per cent at Chittagong in January. The rainy season by contrast is very unpleasant with high relative humidity (86·5 per cent at Chittagong in July) accompanying quite high temperatures. For most of the rainy season cloudy conditions prevail in marked contrast to the rest of the year. The sunshine data for Calcutta may be taken as representative of nearby Bangladesh. Figure 3.1 shows the percentage of the possible sunshine recorded each month at Calcutta. It should be appreciated that uncomfortably hot humid weather persists into October despite the return of sunny skies, since temperatures remain high, and following the

TABLE 3.1

TABLE 3.1
Average monthly maximum and minimum temperature (°C)

		Jan.	Feb.	March	April	May	June	July	Aug.	Sept.	Oct.	Nov.	Dec.
Dinajpur	Max.	24	26	32	34	33	32	32	32	32	31	28	24
	Min.	9	12	16	21	23	25	26	26	26	22	16	11
Chittagong	Max.	26	28	31	32	32	31	30	30	31	31	29	26
	Min.	13	15	19	23	24	25	25	24	24	23	19	14

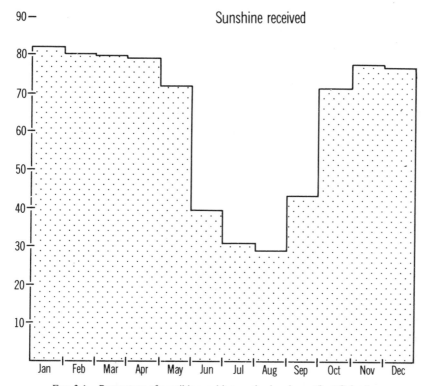

FIG. 3.1   Percentage of possible sunshine received each month at Calcutta.

months of rain and flood there is usually a super-abundance of standing water contributing moisture to maintain an unpleasantly 'sticky' atmosphere.

WINDS

Bangladesh is characterised by light winds or calms as a rule but occasionally damaging storms occur. The notoriously devastating cyclones that periodically harass the coastal districts are discussed further below. More frequent but fortunately less severe hazards for the farmer are associated with the 'nor'westers' of March and April. Strong local winds occasionally occurring as tornadoes can cause damage to the frailly structured Bengali homestead, but more substantial losses are incurred as a result of hail accompanying such storms. In Sylhet hail is particularly feared by the tea planters, as it strips the young leaves and shoots from the bushes at a vital stage of their development at the beginning of the plucking season. In the western districts hail at this time may damage ripening wheat, fruiting mangoes and the mulberry leaves on which the silk industry depends. Hail storms may occur at other times also, being particularly serious if the main aman paddy crop is laid, causing loss of yields and increased costs of reaping. Phenomenal hail storms have even been known to kill livestock.

RAINFALL

Although the map of mean annual rainfall (Fig. 3.2) indicates a range of total rainfall extending from under *c.* 1500 mm (60 in.) in the west to over *c.* 3000 mm (120 in.) in Sylhet and southern Chittagong, the rainfall régime is remarkably similar throughout the country. The dispersion diagrams (Fig. 3.2) and Table 3.2 indicate this clearly. In the table the average rainfall in the three seasons commonly recognised is shown by amount and percentage of the annual total at the five places for which dispersion diagrams are given. The latter show for each month the absolute maximum and minimum recorded (over a period of twenty-five years), the median value (i.e. that above and below which there is an equal number of records) and the interquartile range. One quarter of the readings lie above the upper quartile, one quarter below the lower quartile, with half the readings within the interquartile range (I.Q.R.). Thus the I.Q.R. can be read to mean that as often as not the rainfall will lie within this range.

The monthly rainfall medians for these five stations are tabulated in Table 3.3. (As a rough measure of the minimum needs of rainfall to sustain a rice crop without irrigation, 12·5 mm (0·5 in.) per week (or 50 mm (*c.* 2 in.) per month) may be used.) This is a very crude guide, since there will be greater needs at the time the land is being prepared, especially if the soil is dry, and conversely towards harvest time less direct rainfall may be needed if the soil moisture level is adequate from earlier precipitation. Crop requirements will vary also with the temperature and with the nature of the soil. Evapo-transpiration of moisture by the crop and the soil surface basically increases with air temperature from a minimum in December to more than double the rate by March.

Permeable soils will allow water to pass through them while impermeable clays may store water longer within reach of plant roots. The yield level of the crop should also be taken into account. A crop growing under optimum conditions needs much more water than is required merely to sustain it alive. Research has shown that even with only half the water the plant needs to produce its optimum yield, two-thirds of this level of production can be achieved. The 'minimum need' represented by 50 mm (2 in.) rainfall per month may be taken as lying some way below the optimum requirement.

From Table 3.3 it is clear that with the possible exception of Cox's Bazar in November and Sylhet in March, the drought of the five-month period of the dry season is too severe for rain-fed paddy cultivation. Over most of Bangladesh, November, December and January are almost completely rainless. Occasional storms make possible a recordable median rainfall in February and March, but variability is still very high (Table 3.4).

What little rain may fall in March and in the succeeding two months is attributable, in the main, to the thundery squalls locally known as 'nor'-westers' but liable to blow from other quarters also.

The monthly variability is calculated as the proportion, expressed as a percentage, of half the interquartile range to the median value. In Fig. 3.3 the average rainfall during the five-month dry season is mapped to show the longitudinal pattern of the isohyets; the west, with under 75 mm (*c.* 3 in.), is twice as dry as the east. In agricultural terms all this means is that the farmers in the eastern half of the country stand a rather better chance than their western cousins, as far as rainfall goes, of being able to start preparing land in March.

April and May together constitute the '*Chota Barsat*' or the season of the 'little rains'. Monthly

TABLE 3.2

Rainfall by seasons

	Dry season Nov.–March		Little rains ('Chota Barsat') April–May		Rainy season June–Oct.		Total for year
	mm	%	mm	%	mm	%	mm
Dinajpur	54	3	253	13	1641	84	1948
Jessore	114	7	295	18	1199	75	1608
Dacca	122	6	381	20	1372	74	1875
Sylhet	194	6	711	22	2339	72	3244
Cox's Bazar	158	5	445	12	2972	83	3575

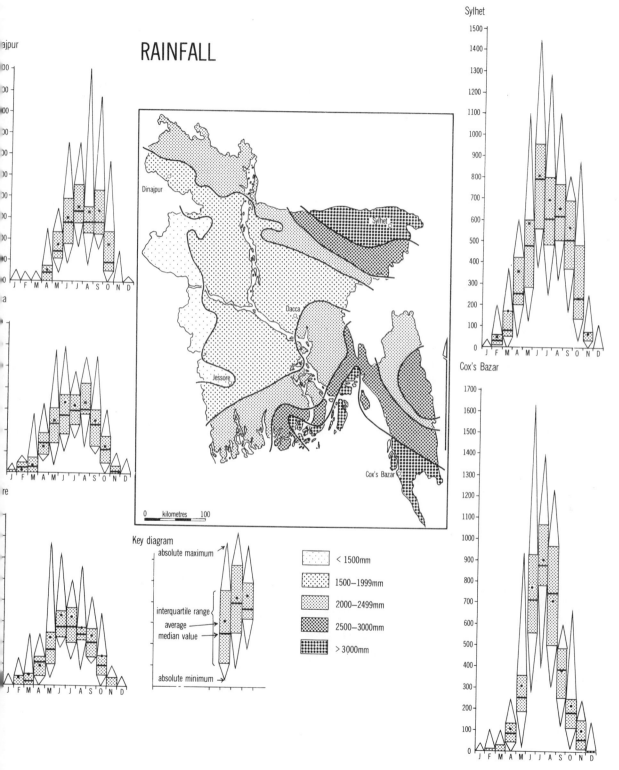

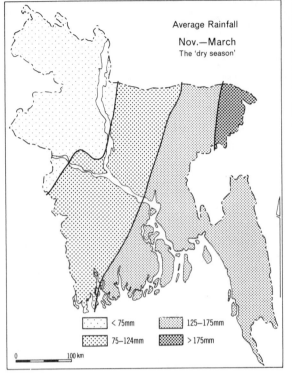

FIG. 3.3 (*a*)   The dry season.

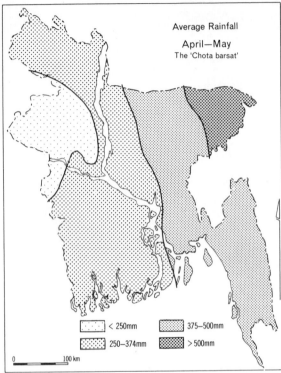

FIG. 3.3 (*b*)   The *chota barsat* or little rains.

FIG. 3.3 (*c*)   The rainy season.

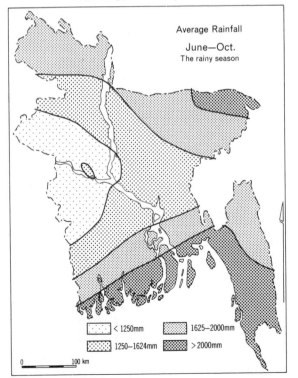

FIG. 3.3   Seasonal Rainfall.

TABLE 3.3

Monthly rainfall medians (in mm)

	Dry season					'Chota Barsat'		Rainy season						
	Nov.	Dec.	Jan.	Feb.	March	April	May	June	July	Aug.	Sept.	Oct.	Nov.	Dec.
Dinajpur	0	0	3	51	3	51	165	279	330	279	279	76	0	0
Jessore	0	0	0	13	23	102	152	279	279	241	203	76	0	0
Dacca	3	0	3	28	36	142	229	279	304	304	229	102	3	0
Sylhet	8	0	0	20	64	254	292	762	610	635	508	229	8	0
Cox's Bazar	51	0	0	5	3	102	241	711	889	762	381	178	51	0

variability is seen to drop substantially compared with March and the median totals exceed the notional minimum for rainfed agriculture. However, the use of monthly totals for April disguises the fact that the probability of rainfall increases through the month, and that an apparently adequate total for the month may come from an abundant fall in the last week, following three weeks of continued dry weather. Studies of rainfall probability indicate that the weekly requirement of 12·5 mm (0·5 in.) will be met at least one year in two by the third week in April in Dacca and the northeast, and by the first week in May in the far west. These probability studies suggest an even chance of adequate rainfall for a total growing season starting at the times indicated of 27–28 weeks in the east, 25–26 weeks in most western areas and 23 weeks at Rajshahi. Like the map of rainfall during the 'chota barsat' (Fig. 3.3b) the westerly decrease in growing period repeats the longitudinal pattern of the dry season isohyets. The extreme variability of the little rains is of very real concern to the cultivator and it is important to stress that 'even chances' of adequate rainfall for cultivation are still gamblers' terms rather than those desired by investors in a commercial proposition. The chances improve eastwards. In the monthly rainfall dispersion diagrams (Fig. 3.2) the position of the lower quartile is another measure of the risk of drought. One year in four at Cox's Bazar and Jessore, the April precipitation is less than 50 mm (2 in.) and at Dinajpur less than 12·5 mm (0·5 in.). Data for a total of thirteen stations suggest that only in the northeast quarter of the country, including Dacca, Mymensingh, Sylhet and Comilla, does the lower quartile for April stand above 50 mm (2 in.).

May shows a distinct improvement over April with the lower quartile in all stations over 66 mm (2·6 in.). Yet another indicator of drought probability is the likelihood of there being less than 50 mm (2 in.) rainfall in a 30-day period. Within the two month period, March–April, such a deficiency is the normal expectancy. In May–June, it happens one year in five in Barisal and Rajshahi, one year in ten at most stations other than those near to the northern hills (e.g. Rangpur, Mymensingh, Comilla).

By early June the likelihood of there being less than 25 mm (1 in.) of rain in a fortnight is less than one chance in ten at all stations except Rajshahi. June–July–August and September can be regarded as adequately rainy months as a rule. Figure 3.3c shows the rainfall pattern for June–October. Though there may be breaks in the rains these are rarely long enough to allow the soil moisture to be seriously reduced. By October however variability around the minimum rainfall for crop growth again becomes significant, and a lower quartile of less than 50 mm (2 in.) for the month is recorded for the western stations of Dinajpur, Pabna, Rajshahi and Jessore, and for Dacca in the centre.

The maps in Fig. 3.4 show the average rainfall in October alongside that for 1935, a year with a particularly short monsoon. Only the extreme northeast and southeastern parts of the country received more than 50 mm (2 in.).

Enough evidence has been presented to support the observation of a noted Bangalee geographer and sociologist Radhakamal Mukerjee, who wrote that 'rainfall in the months from March to May and again from September and October rather than the total, determines the fortunes of the agriculturalist'.

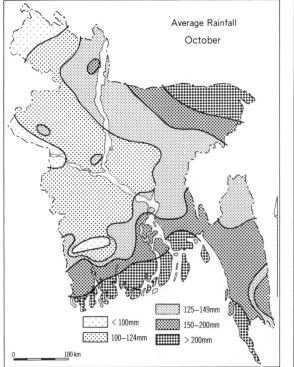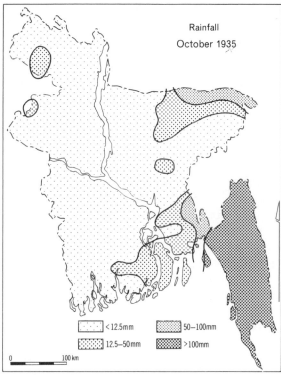

FIG. 3.4   October rainfall: the average (*a*) compared with (*b*) October 1935,
when the rainy season stopped early.

TABLE 3.4
Monthly rainfall variability

	Nov.	Dec.	Jan.	Feb.	March	April	May	June	July	Aug.	Sept.	Oct.	Nov.	Dec.
Dinajpur	∞	∞	200	275	275	60	45	38	34	29	40	113	∞	∞
Jessore	∞	∞	∞	150	122	45	51	23	29	13	38	50	∞	∞
Dacca	575	∞	250	91	102	36	36	32	23	25	39	62	575	∞
Sylhet	333	∞	100	94	100	41	32	29	25	21	33	72	333	∞
Cox's Bazar	175	∞	∞	150	430	55	39	28	16	31	32	150	175	∞

CHAPTER FOUR

NATURAL HAZARDS

In the previous chapter the uncertainty of adequate rainfall occurring at the beginning of the rainy season and again towards its end, was seen as a constraint upon agricultural activity, and can be regarded as a natural hazard. However, in the sense that they may be more cataclysmic events, cyclones and floods are the most damaging natural hazards that occur in Bangladesh.

CYCLONES

The coastal regions are subject to damaging cyclones almost every year. Because of the high density of population occupying a flat deltaic area north of the funnelling tidal estuaries, the loss of human life has at times been very great. In November 1970 one cyclone is thought to have killed over half a million people.

Cyclones occur in the Bay of Bengal chiefly in two seasons; April–May and October–November. They originate as depressions in sea areas to the east, in the South China Sea for example, and intensify into tropical cyclones as they progress into the Bay of Bengal. Some strike across peninsular India to cause havoc in the Arabian Sea. Many adopt a curvilinear path within the Bay, developing from a westerly to a more northerly track (Fig. 4.1a). Thus the coast of Andhra Pradesh and Orissa receive frequent cyclones from the southeast quarter. The cyclones that menace Bangladesh have curved still further to approach the estuary of the Meghna from the S.S.W. and the Chittagong coast from the southwest. Over land, cyclones are soon dissipated as they move away from the water body which is their energy source.

Characteristically a tropical cyclone is of relatively limited areal extent compared with a de-

pression in temperate latitudes, consisting of an intensively low pressure centre around which winds circulate in an anti-clockwise direction (in the northern hemisphere) at very high speeds. Wind velocities in excess of 160 km.p.h. (100 m.p.h.) are not unusual, and in recent severe cyclones since 1960 193 km.p.h. (120 m.p.h.) was recorded in five. The most devastating cyclone in living memory, on 12 November 1970, may have developed winds of 241 km.p.h. (150 m.p.h.). Much higher velocities have been recorded in Pacific cyclones, so the

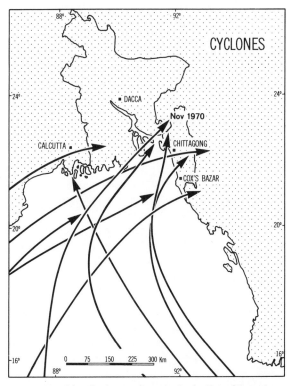

FIG. 4.1 (a)   Cyclone trajectories in the Bay of Bengal.

Bangladesh data may be accepted as reasonable estimates.

In a country where the majority of the people live in bamboo and timber-framed huts, walled with matting and thatched with grass or palm leaves, a large proportion of dwellings is flattened by even a moderate cyclone. However the greater destructive force of cyclones in Bangladesh comes from the storm surge engendered by the strong winds. A wave of up to 9 m (30 ft) high was produced by the cyclone of November 1970. Its devastating effect was very greatly increased by the fact that the storm swept up the gently shelving shores of the estuarine channels at a period of high tide. The tidal range at Sandwip Island is 4 m (13 ft) and along the Noakhali coast 3·4 m (11 ft). In combination the storm surge and tidal wave became a formidable wall of water carried forward by the hurricane force wind to overwhelm the riverain islands and low coastal plains, later to withdraw like a receding wave carrying debris and the dead, humans and animals, out to the sea.

The following quotation from a study on the assessment of cyclone relief needs by two cholera research workers vividly describes the situation:

'Villagers described the flooding in one of two ways, depending on their location: either as a gradual process increasing over hours until it reached a height of 8 to 20 feet, or as a sudden thunderous roar followed by a massive wall of water. Whichever the onset, the results were the same: huge numbers of deaths, all within the brief period of a single night. Where the water rose gradually, people scrambled on to roofs of their houses or scaled trees. But the houses frequently gave way, and only the strongest could maintain their grip on the wet and slippery tree trunks in the face of the 90-mile-per-hour winds. In areas where the tidal bore struck suddenly, there was even less hope of withstanding the force of the waves. After the water receded, those not washed out to sea were often found miles inland, caught in the branches of some distant tree.

'The mortality was appalling. Almost 17 per cent of the population of the surveyed area, at least 225,000 people in all, were lost in the storm. This is far from the total. We had no accurate way of estimating the losses among migrant workers, between 100,000 and 500,000 of whom had come

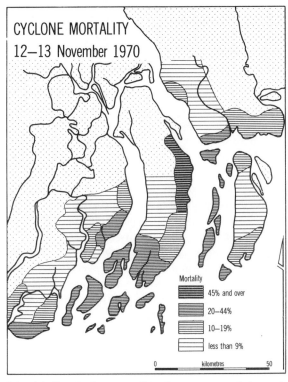

Fig. 4.1 (*b*)   Cyclone mortality: the percentage of the total population estimated dead in the coastal belt of Patuakhali and Noakhali Districts. The largest island in the centre of the map is Bhola. (Based on a map in 'Disaster in Bangladesh', courtesy O.U.P., New York.)

south to help with the harvest, and all of whom slept in the low-lying fields without benefit of houses or trees.

'Mortality varied considerably with geography. On such off-shore islands as Char Hare and Sonar Char it reached 100 per cent, and all that remained of large pre-cyclone settlements were some trees and an occasional dirt mound.'* (See Fig. 4.1*b*.)

The impact of the cyclone of November 1970 was particularly severe in that it came during harvest time, when many thousands of itinerant seasonal labourers were camping in the region to cut the aman crop. The harvest itself was largely ruined, as was the prospect of again cultivating the fields until after a season of rains could wash the sea water out of the soil.

* Sommer, Alfred and Mosley, W. Henry 'The Cyclone: Medical assessment and determination of relief and rehabilitation requirements', in Chen, Lincoln C. (Ed.) 'Disaster in Bangladesh', O.U.P. New York 1973.

The particular cyclone described above differed only in degree from those that occur at least once annually in the region. Those who live in developed countries may well find it difficult to believe that people will persist in living under the threat of such a hazard. Studies were made in the 1960s following a succession of cyclones in 1960–61 to ascertain how the local population regarded the risks which hung over their heads through every spring and autumn, and how they adapted to these conditions. Dr. Aminul Islam found that the majority felt there was little they could do since a cyclone was an 'Act of God'. Migration from the area of risk was out of the question for most, since their livelihood was the land. In fact over the years population had increased in cyclone-threatened areas both by natural excess of births over deaths, and by in-migration of settlers to newly reclaimed coastal tracts. An area of 202,300 ha (500,000 acres) was newly settled in Noakhali District and perhaps double this area reclaimed from the bed of the Meghna by embankment across its minor channels close to the Noakhali bank. Pressure of population on the land in an overpopulated country is a strong incentive to settle new land even in the face of natural hazards. A fatalistic attitude may be man's ultimate adjustment to forces with which he seems too puny to contend.

However, it has been shown that in most cyclones in Bangladesh not more than 10 per cent of the population perish in the region affected, and these are likely to be mainly the very young, the aged and the infirm, i.e. those incapable of fending for themselves in the final crisis of the arrival of the storm surge, by climbing trees. Individual households may take precautions against the risks by constructing raised platforms in their huts or even by constructing earthen mounds fenced and in part roofed over to accommodate stock and people during exceptional floods and high tides. Sure protection against the strongest cyclone is beyond the means of the cultivator. For him and his family hope lies in an early warning of a threatened cyclone to enable them to evacuate to a place of greater safety, and should this be impossible the chance of keeping above water on the floating roof of their house, on a casually constructed raft, or *in extremis* by climbing a stout palm tree and tying themselves to it while the surge passes. For all these eventualities some forethought may be taken in the long term, in the design of the house roof, the planting of suitable trees, etc. His livestock, unless there is a safety mound, have to fend for themselves and will generally be swept away to drown.

The community at large has access to resources and knowledge beyond the reach of the individual peasant, and despite the catastrophe of November 1970 the possibility for minimising loss of life had been much increased over the previous decade. At the international level weather satellites now regularly scan the area and their pictures are received in Dacca and in Washington, U.S.A. The existence of the 1970 cyclone and its severity were recognised in advance, and the rate of its progress could be observed by the radar installation set up for the purpose at Cox's Bazar. It was the more difficult procedure for communicating by radio the imminence of danger to the mass of the population that broke down. Granted a warning system that can give people eight hours in which to act, many could remove themselves to the community refuges constructed to serve several villages. The refuges are two-storey buildings accommodating 500 people and equipped with fresh water tanks at a level intended to escape saline pollution by the storm surge.

Absolute security against cyclone hazard is probably out of the question except for objectives of very limited size. Normal embankments with sluices to protect low areas from a 3 m (10 ft) tidal influx cost around Taka 180,000 ($U.S. 25,000) per mile; protection against storm surge would cost probably more than ten times this sum, a prohibitive expenditure if measured against the value of production so insured. So far it appears no government agency has succeeded in setting out a balance sheet of the social and economic costs of cyclone disaster against the costs of protection against it. While land and alternative sources of livelihood remain scarce in Bangladesh, the authorities are unlikely to be able, even if willing, to declare uninhabitable the areas of hazard. Where man normally lives so close to the margin of bare subsistence, 'living dangerously' under the threat of periodic storm surge and hurricane wind is less of a deterrent to settlement than it might be in an economically advanced country.

RIVERS AND FLOODS

In most countries floods are regarded as hazards with which the population have to contend from time to time as with other disasters, natural and man-made. In Bangladesh, flooding is very much a part of the normal cycle of the seasons. A delta cannot develop physically without flooding, and it is to floodwaters bearing plant nutrients in the form of dissolved and suspended solids that much of a delta's fertility can be attributed. Man has therefore been attracted to the sometimes hazardous environment of the delta because of the returns in terms of food crops that it is able to give him. Traditional agriculture in Bangladesh is an adaptation to a régime of annual deluge by the monsoon rains and floods both from this rain and from the over-spilling of the rivers. Modernisation of agriculture requires that man be less directly at the mercy of natural events, and better able to control all the factors of production. The Bangalee farmer hopefully moving towards a more scientific agriculture has still to adapt the modern technology he is becoming aware of, to the same vagaries of nature as faced his father. In the case of flood control the scale of the problem is generally beyond the individual's power to attempt to do anything about it and he looks to the greater financial and technical resources of his Government and of richer, more advanced countries to seek a solution. So in considering floods in Bangladesh, we have to strike a balance sheet between floods as a hazard and floods as an asset, between floods drowning crops and livestock, and damaging property, and floods watering and fertilising the land.

Bangladesh has a superabundance of water if one sets the amount that can be used by crops against the quantity that flows into the country from outside and falls on its surface as rain. Rather more than four times as much water flows *into* as falls *on* Bangladesh.

Unfortunately local rainfall is highly concentrated into about half of the year when rivers are also at their height. (See Table 3.2.) In brief the problem is to regulate or adapt to the surplus of the rainy season and to husband and use efficiently the scarce resources of water in the dry season. Ultimately it may prove feasible to regulate the flow in the major rivers by works in their headwaters, but this will depend on close international co-operation between India, Bangladesh and probably China, not to mention the expenditure of enormous amounts of capital.

Travelling through or flying over the lowlands during July or August one sees 'water, water, everywhere', even when the rivers are not in full flood. With precipitation in July, for example, averaging around 13 mm (half an inch) daily it can be appreciated that rainfall alone can account for the flooding of vast areas of near level land.

It is commonly the case that local surface water cannot drain away because of ponding back of the minor tributaries by floodwaters in the major rivers. Severe flooding occurs when the latter, carrying water from catchment areas outside Bangladesh, overtop their levees and add their excess to the existing depth of accumulated local rainfall.

The régimes of the Ganges, Brahmaputra–Jamuna and Meghna Rivers are shown in Fig. 4.2. The régimes are basically similar in showing a rapid rise to a peak and a somewhat gentler fall to a pre-monsoon minimum, but there are significant minor differences. The Meghna flow rises early to a maximum in late May and June. This is partly explained by the comparatively short distance the river has to flow compared with the other larger rivers, and partly by the earlier rainfall in the Assam Hills. Consequently the Meghna Depression fills with water by May and remains a great lake until October when the level of the Meghna at the outflow of the depression near the recording point at Bhairab Bazar begins to fall. The Brahmaputra–Jamuna rises more gradually to a July peak, while the Ganges reaches its peak in August from a minimum in April–May, differences that reflect the later onset of the monsoon rains in the Ganges catchment compared with the easterly areas drained by the Brahmaputra.

Figure 4.3 summarises the situation as regards flooding. Less than a half of the country (including the hill areas) can be regarded as flood free; one third floods annually and of this probably a third is inundated to a depth of a metre (3 ft) or more. The agriculturalist has traditionally come to terms with flooding of this order by growing rice varieties that can grow tall and rapidly to keep their heads above water. Many of the highest yielding varieties of rices now being made available to the cultivator cannot survive being drowned for more than three

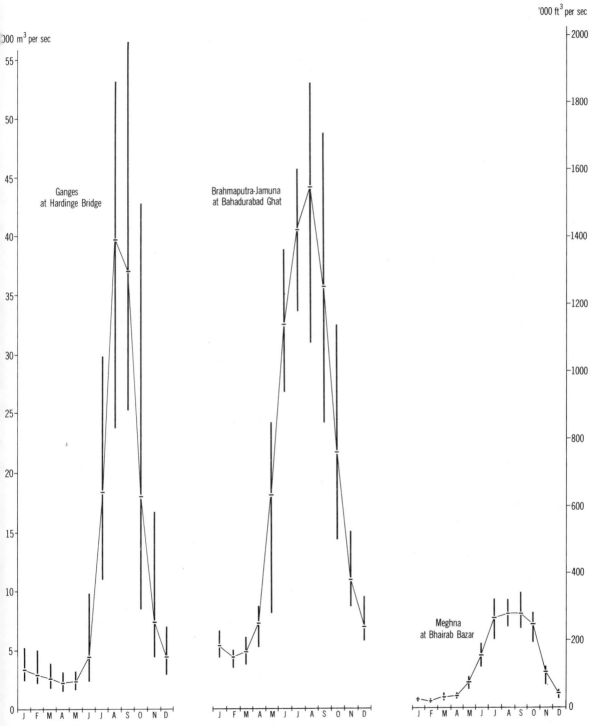

FIG. 4.2 Régimes of the major rivers. The vertical bars indicate the range of discharge for each month, the cross bar the mean rate. Note the very low rates of flow, particularly in the Ganges during the dry season.

to five days. A major challenge faces the engineers who with limited resources have to design, execute and maintain flood protection works to enable the mass of the farmers to enjoy the economic benefits of the high yielding varieties.

The map of flooded areas (Fig. 4.3) should be compared with that of the generalised physiographic types. It will be seen that the areas generally free from annual floods (except of course those due to occasional local downpours) are the hill country of Chittagong and Sylhet, the North Bengal Sandy Alluvial Fan and the Barind. In a sense the Tidal Delta is free of deep-standing floods, but it certainly experiences widespread shallow flooding and infrequent but devastating cyclonic storm surges. Much the same is true of the Noakhali–Chittagong plains though in many places floods exceed 1 m (3 ft) in depth. Flooding of moderate depth only, occurs in the Ganges left-bank levee plains in Rajshahi and the Moribund Delta in the southwest. Other regions of moderate flooding flank the Brahmaputra–Jamuna and extend into the Madhupur Tract and the Old Brahmaputra flood plain.

In most of these areas effective flood protection can probably be achieved and in fact is being provided in several instances, such as the Brahmaputra Right Bank Embankment Project. The same is probably true of the areas in which more than half the land floods to the 'moderate' depth of over 1 m (3 ft). These are of two kinds. Between the Barind and the Ganges left-bank levees the Atrai River follows what is possibly a tectonic depression, but which also has the nature of a backswamp zone. South of the Ganges–Padma this zone continues in the Stabilised Floodplain and Faridpur Bil which floods in part from the Ganges. The Tippera Surface floods in some measure from the Meghna, but more hazardous are the flash floods from the Gumti that drains from the hills of Indian Tripura.

The regions of severe flooding are most extensive in the Meghna Depression of Sylhet and

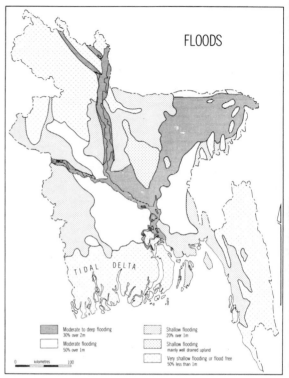

FIG. 4.3 Floods. An attempt is made here to indicate the relative severity of flooding by showing the proportion of the area regularly inundated to a given depth.

Mymensingh, and along the Meghna flood plain from Bhairab Bazar to the confluence with the Padma. Here this deeply flooded zone is continuous with another paralleling the Padma along the Dhaleswari which carries Brahmaputra–Jamuna water past Dacca to the Meghna. In the case of the Meghna Depression, probably no general amelioration can be looked for since the scale of the problem is so great. For some parts of the area it may be worthwhile to construct 'submersible' embankments, designed to be overtopped by maximum floods, but capable of delaying the onset of deep water in the fields, so guaranteeing to the farmer a longer growing season.

CHAPTER FIVE

TRADITIONAL AGRICULTURE

MOUTHS TO FEED: THE BASIC PROBLEM

By 1973 Bangladesh had probably between 75 and 78 million mouths to feed, needing for their monotonously starchy diet about 439 g (15·5 oz) of food grains per day – a total of 13·5 million t (13·3 million lgt) in the year. There was expected to be shortfall of at least 2·5 million lgt, 19 per cent of requirements. While some of the deficiency may be attributed to the disruptions during the war and following independence, which have delayed the effective utilisation of what agricultural innovations were planned, food shortage has been a chronic condition of the country for many years. Imports have run at over 1 million tons of food grains (rice and wheat) annually since 1966–67 and have never been less than 350,520 t (345,000 lgt) since 1960–61. The simple explanation is that production never catches up with demand as the population persists in multiplying at a rate thought to exceed 3 per cent per year.

The immediate problem is to feed the hungry with at least enough to keep them alive. When that is done there remains the long task of improving the diet. The normal intake of food of the average Bangalee gives him 8332 kilo-Joules per day. This diet, while it may be close in energy terms to the 8951 kJ estimated as needed by the present-day Bangalee, having regard to his height and weight, is badly distributed in that too little protein, especially animal protein, is taken. Bangalees are therefore, on average, undernourished and many suffer various forms of malnutrition, particularly of protein deficiency. Probably in 45 per cent of households the average diet regularly provides less than 8951 kJ daily.

A nutrition survey carried out in 1962–64 confirmed these basic facts, and showed the variations in diet as between rural and urban groups, and between poor and well-to-do families. The tables below give averaged data for members of rural and urban families, and for the extremes of economic conditions in both cases.

The basic daily diet of the Bangalee can be summarised thus:

7.   Grain silo near Narayanganj, for storing imported foodstuffs.

Breakfast: rice left over from the previous day's meals, often taken mixed with pulses as a soup. *Chapatti* or *paratha* (unleavened wheat pancake cooked dry or with fat) or a gruel of powdered pulses with *gur* (crude sugar) may take the place of rice.

Midday: rice with a vegetable or fish curry, chillies and onion. Rarely a meat curry. The vegetable will generally be some variety of gourd, potato or leafy green vegetable.

Evening: as midday.

Urban living improves the intake of protein foods, fats and fruit for both rich and poor, the main difference due to economic status being in the much greater consumption of high-protein foods by the well-to-do. In rural areas protein foods are less readily available to either economic group, and the rich are mainly differentiated by the larger quantities of food consumed. The most serious single deficiency in the diet is probably the shortage of Vitamin A, found in fruit and leafy vegetables. In young children (under five) Vitamin A deficiency causes blindness or death in between 0·6 and 0·8 per cent of the age group. A rice diet lacks adequate Vitamins A and C and riboflavin, but

8. Street market: vegetables and spices brought to town by the cultivator.

9. Net-fishing on a tank near Dacca.

these can be made good from pulses. Protein, especially animal protein, is generally deficient, though pulses go some way to provide a reasonable substitute. Protein deficiency in the diet is most common among the low income groups, and it is apparently increasing as pressure on the land to produce rice reduces the area under pulses. Fish is the main source of animal protein, but the fishing industry is in a depressed state for a number of reasons despite its market potential. (See p. 46.)

The dietary Table 5.1 indicates clearly if indirectly the enormous gap that must exist between what food is currently produced and the amount and quality of food which ought to be produced to bring about even a modest improvement in the Bangalee's living standard. Agricultural development programmes, while rightly directed at self-sufficiency in food grains, must not neglect the need to improve the quality of the diet in the interests of producing in the new generation a healthy, intelligent and energetic population.

It is thought feasible for production and consumption of food to come into balance at 19·1 million t (18·8 million lgt) by 1983 when the population would be 101 million. It should be remembered that agriculture must also produce jute for export to earn essential imports of manufacturing goods and agricultural inputs. At present the northwest is the only major region producing a surplus of food, while the south-

west is more or less self-sufficient (Fig. 5.1). The centre of the country, including the Dacca–Naraganganj urban areas and much of the jute area, is most dependent on imported foodstuffs.

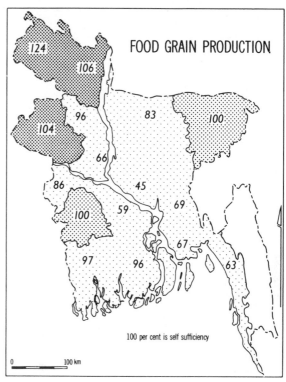

FIG. 5.1   Level of foodgrain self-sufficiency by districts.

(See p. 46.)

TABLE 5.1
Food intake: grams per person per day

	Rural	Rural poorest Rs. 100/month	Rural rich Rs. 500/month	Urban	Urban poor	Urban rich
Cereals	537	506	870	364	326	342
Starchy roots	56	48	94	32	15	46
Sugars, etc.	7	6	56	12	6	17
Pulses, nuts	28	23	54	27	32	18
Vegetables	135	138	171	134	89	129
Fruits	10	5	—	18	12	20
Meats	6	4	—	19	5	38
Eggs	2	1	—	3	2	53
Fish	33	27	38	42	26	54
Milk, cheese	6	10	18	53	16	98
Fats, oils	6	5	15	14	8	22
Spices, etc.	5	5	4	10	—	—
Total	831	778	1320	728	537	837
kJ	9378	8315	15,410	7216	6453	7615
Energy from carbohydrate (%)	83	83·3	84	76	80·7	69·7
from protein (%)	10	10·3	9	11	10·7	11·7
from fat (%)	7	6·4	7	13	8·6	18·6

10. A Bangalee homestead occupied by a 'joint family' of several related adults and their children. Each separate bamboo matting, grass roofed hut is the home of a man, wife and family. Rice which is being dried on mats in the sun is being swept up by the woman in the foreground. Rice straw is stacked beyond. The dark patch on the ground to the left of the children is cow dung being dried for fuel. The trees provide shade and fruit. The light bamboo fence protects a small spice and vegetable garden from goats.

AGRICULTURAL GEOGRAPHY

The land, with its rainfall and its floods, is the principal natural resource of Bangladesh. Human ingenuity, spurred on no doubt by the pressure of population on the increasingly crowded countryside, has brought almost all the surface into productive use. The mainly self-sufficient Bangalee farming family has evolved methods of cropping well adapted to the diverse physiographic conditions of the deltaic lowlands with their seasonal rhythm of drought and flood. Technological advances are helping the cultivator improve his productive capacity. In some instances quite revolutionary changes to his cropping practices may be made possible, but by and large the impact of developments in science and technology is to assist the farmer towards maximising his use of natural resources by improving rather than radically changing the manner of his adaptation to his environment.

The lowland farmer is not purely subsistent. While much of what he grows never leaves the farm and homestead, and is consumed by the family, some crops such as jute are grown entirely to sell, and a proportion of others like tobacco, mustard seed, sugar cane and possibly rice may well be converted to cash.

In the Chittagong Hill Tracts, non-Bangalee people akin to the hill tribesmen of Burma and Assam combine the practice of sedentary agriculture, in the Bangalee style, along the valley bottoms, with *jhum* cultivation, a form of shifting agriculture or 'swidden' farming, on hill slopes.

On the benchlands between hill and plain, fringing the steep slopes in Chittagong District but more particularly in Sylhet, highly efficient tea plantations represent a third distinct type of agricultural development.

FARMING IN THE LOWLANDS

The basic factors influencing the Bangalee farmer in his choice of crop from season to season and from one type of land to another may conveniently be discussed in the context of the chart of agricultural activities (Fig. 5.2). The chart is adapted from the actual cultivation calendar in Iswarganj, a *thana* of Mymensingh District, but it may be taken as a representative model for average conditions in Bangladesh.

Corresponding to the three seasons determined by rainfall incidence and amount, three cropping seasons are recognised:

(i) The *rabi* season corresponds to the dry season, from the end of October to March or April, during which, although only 25 per cent of the cultivated land (*c.* 18 per cent total crop area, T.C.A.) is cropped, a great variety of crops is grown both 'dry' (dependent on moisture remaining in the soil from the wet season) and by irrigation. 'Dry' rabi crops include wheat, oilseeds, pulses, vegetables and tobacco, while boro paddy is by far the most important crop irrigated.

(ii) The *bhadoi* season, during which aus paddy and jute are the main crops cultivated, is literally the rainy season, but in agricultural terms lasts from the 'little rains' or *chota barsat* of the pre-monsoon period from March or April to May until

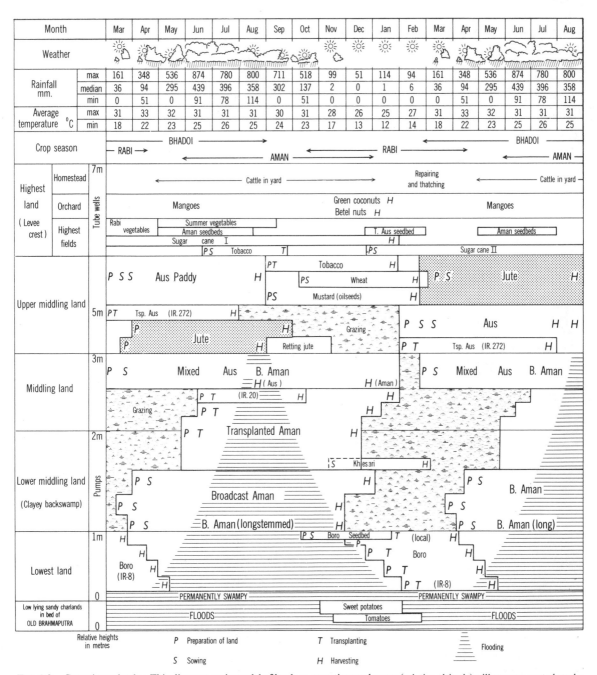

Fig. 5.2 Cropping calendar. This diagrammatic model of land use over time and space (relative altitude) will repay repeated study as you read the text. The seasons and situations in which the H.Y. Varieties of paddy are being used are indicated by the varietal number in brackets. Sugar Cane I and II indicate successive crops each occupying land for 13 months.

11. Gumti River, Comilla; rabi crops along natural levee, flood banks across centre view. Fallow fields, tanks and villages beyond. The Gumti is notorious for its sudden floods.

12. Ploughing on the Dacca–Demra Scheme: a light harrow lies on the bank on the right, behind which runs the irrigation channel.

13. Threshing paddy: muzzled cattle treading out the crop: Cox's Bazar.

14. Threshing by hand, Kushtia District.

these crops are harvested in July or August, at the height of the rainy season.

(iii) The *Aghani* season, more conveniently called the *aman* season, is that of the main rice crops, transplanted and broadcast aman, which may be in the ground from June to November–December. The aman season thus overlaps with both rabi and bhadoi cropping seasons. Little else besides aman paddy is grown.

In any part of the delta (with the exception of the old alluvial terraces) soils differ in texture as between the levee crests (the 'highest land' in the chart) and the backswamp depressions ('lowest land'), often ranging from light sandy loams to heavy clay loams in the space of a few hundred yards and an altitudinal range of a score or so feet. The lighter higher soils are easier to work than those of the heavier lower land, and can often be tilled dry or with the minimum of moistening from early rains in March. Close to the homesteads, for which sites are selected on the highest parts of the levee in order to avoid most floods, vegetables and spices may be grown in kitchen fields all the year round, and a small area of sugar cane cultivated

under fairly close supervision. Seed-beds of tobacco and aman paddy may also be planted here if water is available from a tank or well near by. These lands receive most of what little there is to spare in the way of animal manure after domestic needs for fuel have been satisfied, and their crops are usually fenced to protect them from stray cattle and goats looking for forage. Fruit trees, mangoes, jack fruit, betel nut and coconut-palms shade the homesteads and provide a supplement to the farmer's diet and to his income. Apart from the fields immediately around the homestead, most of the agricultural land is unfenced, and the farmer has little choice but to cultivate his scattered fields in the same way as do his neighbours. So although the village lands may be farmed by a number of individuals, there is little apparent variety to distinguish one plot from another. Normally a farmer holds his lands in a number of separate parcels in different parts of the village, some high some low.

The highest 'open fields' carry aus paddy and jute in the bhadoi season, both crops which rely on direct rainfall for moisture and which prefer not to grow in standing water. Aus paddy is an 'upland'

15. Pulling and bundling paddy seedlings for the transplanted *boro* crop at Demra.

16. Harvesting *aman* paddy at Demra. This is still the normal method throughout Bangladesh.

variety, sown broadcast in non-flooded land. It is harvested in August, when the weather is wet, hot and very humid. Because of its poor keeping qualities, partly related to these conditions, aus rarely enters into trade. Jute is more tolerant of floods, but deteriorates in quality if left long to grow in water. However, the farmer may have to harvest it in water waist-deep if the monsoon rains are exceptionally heavy. After cutting, the jute is retted by soaking in water until the fibres can be stripped from the stem, washed and bundled in skeins for baling in hydraulic presses at collecting centres.

Some of the land that has carried one of the two bhadoi crops may be ploughed during September and sown with mustard to produce seed for cooking-oil before being cultivated in readiness for the next bhadoi season. Tobacco can also be fitted into this period, the seedlings being planted out from the plots nearer the homestead.

On some of the land sown to aus, aman paddy may be broadcast with the aus seed, to mature after the aus has been harvested. This practice is regarded as an insurance against either crop failing, but does not get the best yields of either. Aman may also occasionally be intersown with jute.

In any village, the greater part of the land will probably be 'middling' land or lower. Here aman is the main crop. These lands are generally too heavy for early ploughing, and have first to be thoroughly soaked by the 'little rains'. The best yields come from aman, which is transplanted from seed-beds into rain-flooded fields early in the monsoon. Heavy rains and sometimes river floods keep the paddy-fields thoroughly wet, and the latter introduce soluble plant nutrients as well as essential moisture. Later transplanted crops may need rain in October for best results, after which the fields dry out and the crop ripens to be harvested in the clear sunny days of November–December. A common practice is to sow a pulse, *khesari*, among the ripening aman so obtaining a useful 'catch' crop for food and fodder early in the dry season.

On lower land the risk of flooding is naturally greater, and consequently broadcast varieties of aman are sown, among them long-stemmed types. Preparation of land for broadcasting aman can be more cursory than for transplanting, and the object is to get the aman plant well established before the onset of floods, so that the plant can grow quickly when the floods come, keeping its head above the rising water. Aman can grow at the rate of at least an inch a day, some varieties as much as 30 cm (12 in.) in twenty-four hours. The long-stemmed aman can produce a stalk 7 m (23 ft) long, and often has to float in water 4·5 m (15 ft) deep. As the floods recede the stalk subsides and puts out rootlets from its 'joints'.

Where the combined 'little' and monsoon rains last long enough, it is sometimes possible to follow aus with aman on the same land, but the presence of both crops in a farming system usually means they are grown on different fields.

The lowest land of all, in the backswamp depression, may flood too soon for aman to be grown, but is in some areas cultivated as soon as the flood-waters (or accumulated local rain-water) have receded enough to allow a plough team to work knee-deep in water and mud. The dry season *boro* paddy is transplanted before the fields dry out, and has to be irrigated throughout the rainless months of January and February. Water scoops operated on the cantilever principle, water shovels, and baskets swung on ropes are used to raise water from the dwindling backswamp lake, into which the boro fields advance as the water recedes. Low-lift diesel pumps are becoming widely used to increase the efficiency of boro production, and it may be advantageous to speed the initial cultivation by tractor ploughing since the secret of success is to make the most of the water left over after the end of the rains before it evaporates. Although it is nutritious and yields well, growing in the clear dry season sunshine, boro paddy is relatively coarse and not popular in trade.

A final element in the chart is grazing. Cattle and water buffalo are used in ploughing, and to a small extent as milking animals. During the dry season the beasts are grazed communally on the paddy stubble, but while aus or aman crops are in the open fields they have to be fed near the homesteads on rice-straw or grass cut and carried by the children.

The Regional Pattern of Crops
While the local diversity of physiographic site in relation to soil texture and water is reflected generally in diversity of crops and cropping practices

17. Raising water by bucket swinging. The pond is covered with water hyacinth. The boys sit on a bamboo frame and throw the water into a channel protected by banana leaves.

18.   Traditional water scoop or *dunga* used to raise water up to 0·5 metres. The cultivator depresses the righthand end into the pool, raising it again with the help of the counter balanced lever weighted with clay at its lefthand end, thus allowing the water to flow out of the scoop into the field in the foreground.

over short distances, the relative importance of the chief elements in lowland agriculture shows enough areal differentiation to form the basis of a system of crop association regions.

The distribution of the five main crops and a selected group of non-rice rabi crops is shown in Figs 5.3–5.13 which are based mainly on data for 1969–70. In each case these maps show for each thana (the smallest areal unit for agricultural statistics) the proportion of the total cropped area (T.C.A.) (derived from the sum of the six items) represented by the area under the particular crop. The range of values used is based on the quintile distribution of the thana data. Thus one-fifth of the thanas have a given crop occupying a percentage of the total cropped area within the range of each quintile. The pattern of distribution of the six items – aus paddy, jute, transplanted and broadcast aman, boro paddy and 'dry' rabi crops – will be examined in turn as a background to a discussion of generalised agricultural regions. It should be noted that in the Chittagong Hill Tracts only the areas under permanent 'lowland agriculture' are included in the calculation. (See Fig. 6.3.)

Aus

Aus paddy and jute compete for land in the *bhadoi* (rainy) season, being sown during the *chota barsat* of March–April to be harvested at the height of the main rains in July–August. The need to prepare fields to be ready to receive broadcast seed with the onset of the *chota barsat* limits the crop to the lighter soils. Uncertainty of rainfall at this season and the generally more pervious nature of the soils

used prevents the practice of transplanting except where irrigation can be provided. The lighter soils workable for aus cultivation tend as a rule to be on higher ground, within the delta, though more extensive areas of sandy loams are widespread in the North Bengal Sandy Alluvial Fan and in regions deriving sediment from the Brahmaputra, i.e. the Old Brahmaputra Plain in Mymensingh and the

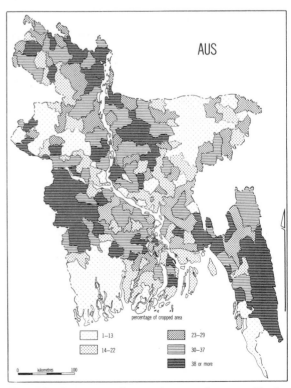

FIG. 5.3   Percentage of cropped area under aus paddy, by thanas.

Brahmaputra–Jamuna flood plain where silty soils maintain reserves of moisture sufficient to allow for early sowing before the rains. These areas all have blocks of thanas where aus exceeds 39 per cent of the T.C.A. (Fig. 5.3). The most substantial area of aus dominance is in the Moribund Delta where loamy clay soils are usual on higher ground. Here dry rabi crops follow.

However, in only 15 of 415 thanas does the crop occupy 50 per cent or more of the T.C.A., and so in thanas within the two upper quintiles where it occupies 30 per cent or more, aus is in combination with other crops on a substantial part of the land. A not infrequent practice is to broadcast the non-photosensitive aus and photosensitive aman together at the time of the *chota barsat* in the expectation of harvesting a short season aus crop before it drowns in the floodwaters early in the rainy season and later in November reaping the crop of deepwater aman when the floods recede. This practice insures the farmer against total failure. Another variety of fast maturing aus is broadcast on charlands in April to be harvested sixty days later in June or July, hopefully before floods and swift currents make any cropping impossible. Some aus is transplanted, but the inability of the crop to keep pace with rising water, and its maximum height of *c.* 1 metre (3–3½ ft) make it

unsuitable for low-lying areas. Much aus in any case is grown traditionally in speculative fashion, in the expectation of partial loss, and the hope that some crop will be garnered to tide the household over till the main aman crop can be harvested. In parts of the Tippera Surface and in northern Chittagong the aus crop precedes transplanted aman.

While aus seldom exceeds half the T.C.A., in only 10 per cent of the thanas does it fail to achieve better than 5 per cent. Such areas are the Saline Tidal Delta and the heart of the Meghna Depression. Growing as it does through a season when the probability of rainfall increases all the time (thus reducing the need for irrigation as the crop's demand for water reaches its peak) and being a relatively short-stemmed rice, prospects are good for substituting for traditional varieties high yielding strains provided a minimum of irrigation can be made available to guarantee the survival of the crop in its early stages.

Jute

The farmer's decision whether to include jute in his cropping programme for the bhadoi season is strongly influenced by his estimate of the economic profitability of jute set against his perception of the short-term subsistence needs of his family for rice. Jute is more tolerant than aus of some degree of

19.   Cutting jute near Dacca. The harvest takes place during the wet season, and it is not uncommon for the farmer to have to work waist-deep in flood water.

flooding but demands more nutrient from the soil. It is therefore an appropriate crop on charlands and floodplain lands where soils are easily worked in the dry season and have their nutrient level restored by annual floods. The distribution of thanas in the upper quintile, where jute occupies more than 10 per cent of the T.C.A., picks out such areas along the Brahmaputra–Jamuna, the Old Brahmaputra continuing into the Meghna, and the Ganges–Padma distributaries, the Madhumati and Arial Khan (Fig. 5.4). As revealing of the requirements of the crop is the character of the considerable tracts where jute fails to achieve 1 per cent of the T.C.A. The whole of the lowest quintile of thanas is in this category. Thus the Tidal Delta, particularly the saline portions, Chittagong and parts of the Barind whose soils do not enjoy the benefit of rejuvenating floods, and Sylhet where the floodwaters which come from tributaries to the upper Meghna system carry little nutrient by comparison with Brahmaputra or Ganges water.

Because the ratio of aus to jute varies somewhat with the prospective price of jute and the state of

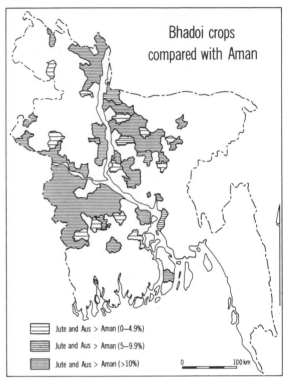

FIG. 5.5 Areas where the area under the *bhadoi* crops, aus and jute, exceeds that under aman paddy, by thanas and percentage excess.

rice stocks on the farm it is helpful to combine their acreages and to note the regions within which they exceed the area under the combined aman crops. This gives an impression of the area where bhadoi season cultivation tends to dominate over that in the main cropping period of the later rains and early dry season. Figure 5.5 shows areas where aus and jute together exceed the combined aman total. It reinforces the conclusions drawn from the separate discussion of the aus and jute distributions.

Aman

The two aman crops are in a distributional sense complementary. While they grow at approximately the same season, they normally occupy different types of land. Many varieties of broadcast aman can tolerate moderate flooding, and some particularly long-stemmed types are adapted to 'floating' in deep water and can grow 25 cm (10 in.) in 24 hours. Traditional transplanted varieties share this ability to grow with rising floodwaters, though in a more modest degree. Once it is about 1 ft (30 cm) tall trans-

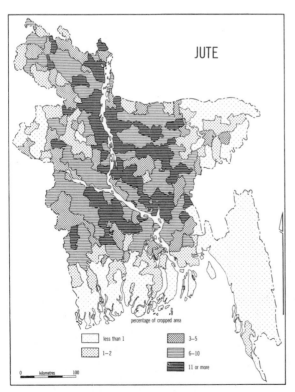

FIG. 5.4 Percentage of cropped area under jute, by thanas.

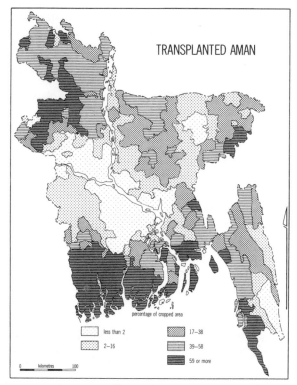

TRANSPLANTED AMAN

percentage of cropped area

	less than 2		17–38
	2–16		39–58
			59 or more

0   kilometres   100

FIG. 5.6   Percentage of cropped area under transplanted aman
paddy by thanas.

planted aman can keep pace with water rising 2·5
cm (1 in.) per day. The aman crops are in the
ground through most of the rainy season and the
periods of maximum flood. The problem to be faced
in substituting high yielding varieties of rice, most
of them shortstemmed, for the traditional long-
stemmed types is examined further below.

Transplanted aman is the preferred main crop
producing the finest quality rice and yielding on
average 18 per cent more than broadcast varieties.
Seed-beds are prepared during the *chota barsat* or
early in the monsoon rains, from which transplantation to the prepared fields takes place in June or
July. Ideally the crop must remain wet until within
three or four weeks of harvest in November–
December. It is thus unsuited to higher sites or
well-drained soils which can suffer from October
drought.

Very high percentages (over 59 per cent) of the
total cropped area are under transplanted aman in
three main areas, in parts of which its cultivation is
almost a monoculture (Fig. 5.6). The Saline Tidal

Delta in Khulna District carries little else but transplanted aman, since it is only after the rains have
washed the salt from the soil to a depth beyond the
crop's roots that the paddy seedlings can be transplanted. The coastal thanas of Patuakhali are
similarly almost monocultural, but inland the percentage under transplanted aman declines. Hatia and
Sandwip Islands and the newly reclaimed charlands
of Ramgati thana in coastal Noakhali have 76 per
cent or more under transplanted aman. With the
onset of the dry season as local freshwater drainage
diminishes, salt water encroaches up the tidal rivers,
and only areas protected by embankments or standing on high ground can carry a rabi crop. Even where
salinity can be avoided or prevented there remains
the problem of finding fresh water to maintain a dry
season crop. Groundwater in the Saline Tidal Delta
is saline and the best prospect lies in bringing in fresh
water from the Ganges, as proposed for the later
phases of the Ganges–Kobadak scheme discussed
below. Cox's Bazar Subdivision in south Chittagong
has very high percentages of land under the crop.
Parts of this area become saline in the dry season
which inhibits general crop diversification, although
boro paddy irrigated from hill streams has become
important in recent years.

A different set of difficulties limits crop diversification and results in very high figures for transplanted aman in the Barind. Here the heavy clay
soils developed on old alluvium cannot be worked
by the light wooden scratch plough drawn by weak
oxen, until softened by rains. Consequently, as in
the saline areas, time allows for the cultivation of a
single rain-fed crop only, and as the region is free
from deep flooding transplanted aman is the
favoured crop. Unlike the saline delta, however, the
Barind is thought to be underlain by reasonably
abundant and accessible fresh groundwater, the
utilisation of which could greatly alter the dry
season face of the region. The clay soils which
prove so intractable when dry make excellent
puddled fields in which sufficient collected rainfall
can be retained in an average year.

Areas where transplanted aman occupies a neg-
ligible proportion of the T.C.A. are mainly those
where broadcast aman flourishes – the more deeply
flooding central region of Bangladesh along the
Ganges–Padma and the low-lying district of
Faridpur. The centre of the Meghna Depression is

also too deeply flooded for transplanted aman, or for broadcast aman for that matter, though to a lesser extent.

Broadcast aman rarely exceeds 70 per cent of the total cropped area (only four thanas) and the base of its upper quintile is at 37 per cent, compared with 59 per cent in the case of transplanted aman (Fig. 5.7). It cannot therefore be regarded as tending towards a monocultural situation except in three quite separate small areas which represent extreme conditions in more extensive regions where it is the dominant crop. Chalan Bil and the associated depression along the Atrai River in Rajshahi and Pabna districts is a region more or less waterlogged throughout the year. Broadcast aman reaches 79 and 82 per cent of T.C.A. in adjacent thanas beyond the southern extremity of the Barind. On either bank of the Ganges–Padma between the Brahmaputra–Jamuna and the Meghna confluences there are broad areas where the thanas are almost all in the upper quintile. The left bank belt, two to three thanas deep – about 30 km (*c.* 20 miles) wide – includes the Dhaleswari anabranch and the

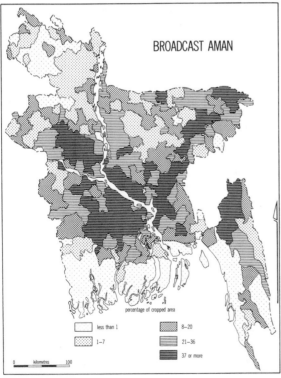

BROADCAST AMAN

percentage of cropped area

less than 1   8–20
1–7   21–36
               37 or more

0   kilometres   100

FIG. 5.7   Percentage of cropped area under broadcast aman paddy by thanas.

Padma backswamps. On the right bank distributaries of the Ganges–Padma, including the Arial Khan, are evidence of the regular flooding of this region which extends south into Faridpur Bil. Again east of the Meghna in a belt practically continuous from northeastern Sylhet (where one thana registers 78 per cent broadcast aman) to the Comilla–Noakhali boundary and averaging about 20 km (*c.* 12½ miles) in width the crop tends to dominate where flooding is moderately but not excessively deep.

The southern part of this zone together with the three areas previously described may be seen to constitute a continuous lowland belt in the centre of the country. Excess of water is the main problem here preventing the introduction of more productive varieties, a problem which can be mitigated, if slowly and only very partially, by flood protection works along the major river.

'Dry' rabi crops

During the dry season, October–November to March–April, cropping depends on moisture remaining in the soil or upon irrigation. For the most part the group of crops referred to as *'dry rabi crops'* have traditionally been grown without irrigation, though improved technology is starting to change the picture. The dry season paddy crop, *boro*, is very dependent on irrigation.

The dry rabi crops as mapped on Fig. 5.8 comprise wheat, oilseeds (mustard, rape, groundnuts), a variety of pulses, tobacco, chillies, potatoes and sugar cane. The latter is included as a rabi crop since it is planted and harvested in the dry season, though occupying land for upwards of twelve months. (Rabi vegetables, onions, garlic and sweet potatoes have not been included because of difficulties in establishing comparisons between the data available at different periods, but together they make up only a small fraction of the total rabi crop, and tend to be fairly ubiquitous.) Of the dry rabi crops under consideration the pulses taken together are most important (exceeding 364,000 ha, 900,000 acres) followed by oilseeds (over 324,000 ha, 800,000 acres, of which mustard has over 202,000 ha, 500,000 acres), wheat (over 121,000 ha, 300,000 acres), potatoes (over 81,000 ha, 200,000 acres), chillies (81,000 ha, 200,000 acres) and tobacco (40,000 ha, 100,000 acres). Sugar cane occupies over 162,000 ha, 400,000 acres.

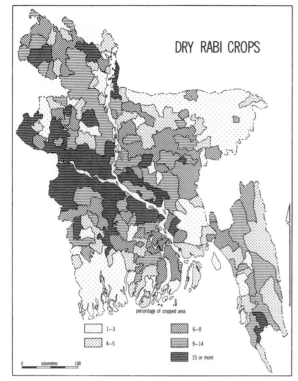

DRY RABI CROPS

percentage of cropped area

1–3   6–8
4–5   9–14
       15 or more

0 kilometres 100

FIG. 5.8   Percentage of cropped area under dry rabi crops by thanas.

The map of dry rabi crops cannot do more than indicate the relative level of importance of the group as a whole since the individual requirements of several crops within the group vary considerably. One of the pulses, khesari, is broadcast on low ground among the ripening aman paddy, while others favour the light soils along the levee ridges. Mustard is tolerant of a wide range of soils, but its cultivation is limited by its association in rotation with aus or jute which it follows on medium to high ground before the end of the rains when lower land is still waterlogged and under aman.

Not a single rural thana has less than 1 per cent of the T.C.A. under dry rabi crops and the median percentage is 8. Domestic subsistence requirements for cooking oil, spices, tobacco, etc., would explain an extensive minimal acreage. High percentages of T.C.A. indicate more commercial objectives to cultivation: for example, there are concentrations of sugar-cane cultivation near to factories in Dinajpur, Rajshahi and Kushtia districts, and of tobacco growing in an area of remarkable specialisation in Rangpur.

The importance of the dry rabi crops in the diet of the Bangalee is much greater than the acreage data might suggest when compared with those for the rice crops. The discussion of diet indicated how vital pulses are as a source of protein. Fats in the diet come mainly from oilseeds such as mustard and groundnuts. It is thus a matter for concern that the area under these groups of crops has failed to keep pace with population growth, and the conclusion can hardly be avoided that the diet is deteriorating as it becomes even more monotonously rice and wheat based.

Pulses (Fig. 5.9), which occupied 0·77 million ha (1·9 million acres) in 1944–45, 0·49 million ha (1·2 million acres) in 1947–48, now fail to reach 0·36 million ha (0·9 million acres). As the maps show, pulses are grown almost everywhere; most areas appearing blank grow small areas. To the extent that there is regional concentration, the light soil areas along the Ganges–Padma and the non-saline tidal delta may be noted. The main areas *not* growing pulses to any great extent are the Barind, the Saline Delta and the Tippera–Chittagong plains. Heavy or seasonally toxic soils, and sheer pressure of population discouraging the cultivation of crops other than rice may be cited as main explanations respectively. The lack of pulses in the Meghna Depression is related to the flood conditions here which delay rabi cropping till well into the cool season.

The areas under oilseed, mustard and groundnuts are mapped in Fig. 5.10. The total area cropped has increased slightly, from 268,400 ha (663,300 acres) in 1947–48 to 303,500 ha (750,000 acres) in 1971–72, but in some recent years has been lower, as in 1969–70 261,000 ha (644,000 acres). The pattern of distribution has changed to become more nearly ubiquitous.

The wheat area (Fig. 5.11) has increased almost fourfold, from 34,400 ha (85,000 acres) in 1947–48 to 120,000 ha (296,200 acres) in 1969–70 and 127,000 ha (314,500 acres) in 1971–72, reflecting the growing popularity of wheat flour especially among the urban population. From a predominantly northwestern pattern of distribution, in the 1940s, wheat cultivation has spread widely, with some concentration in the middle west around the Ganges–Brahmaputra confluence.

Sugar cane (Fig. 5.12) is harvested and planted

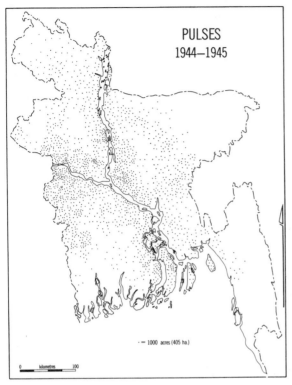

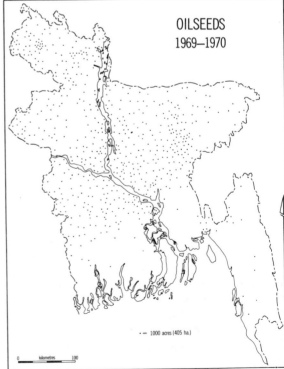

FIG. 5.9   Distribution of the area under pulses (*a*) in 1944–45 and (*b*) in 1969–70.

FIG. 5.10   Distribution of the area under rabi oilseeds (mustard and groundnuts) (*a*) in 1944–45 and (*b*) in 1969–70.

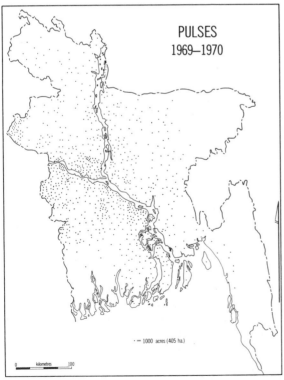

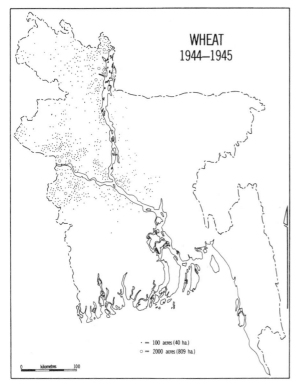

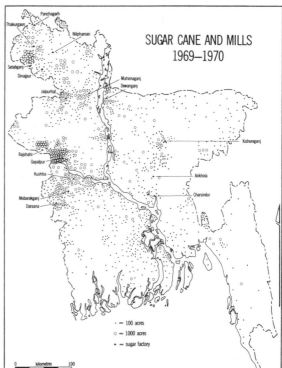

FIG. 5.11 Distribution of the area under wheat (*a*) in 1944–45 and (*b*) in 1969–70.

FIG. 5.12 Distribution of the area under sugar cane and of sugar mills (*a*) in 1944–45 and (*b*) in 1969–70.

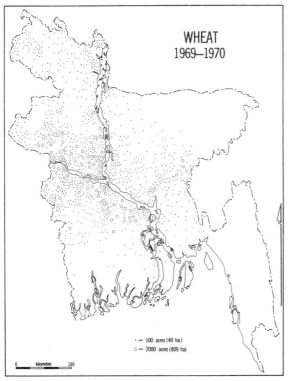

20. Ox- and buffalo-drawn carts bringing sugar cane to Mirpur Railway Station in Kushtia District, for carriage to the sugar mill.

in the cool season. It is grown both as a cash crop to be sold to sugar mills producing refined white sugar, or to smaller entrepreneurs making *gur*, and for home consumption. The pattern of distribution shows concentration around sugar mills against a background of subsistence cultivation in most areas. The area under sugar cane has increased from 91,000 ha (224,400 acres) in 1947–48 to almost 162,000 ha (400,000 acres) in 1969–70.

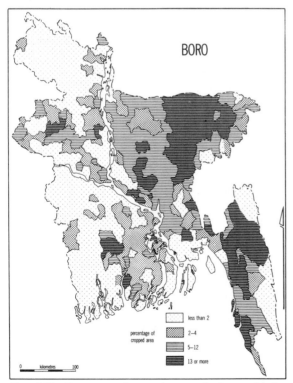

BORO

percentage of cropped area

less than 2
2–4
5–12
13 or more

0   kilometres   100

FIG. 5.13   Percentage of cropped area under boro paddy by thanas.

The success story of *boro paddy* since the introduction of low lift pumps and the high yielding variety IR-8 is elaborated below. Boro has always been a relatively high yielding crop, averaging roughly twice the yield of aman varieties. Dry season sunshine, mild temperatures and relatively low humidity inhibit the development and spread of pests and diseases. Provided a water supply is maintained a good crop of boro can be grown, and with fertiliser and H.Y.V. the yields can be magnificent.

Roughly two types of situation are embodied in Fig. 5.13. Increasingly in recent years, farmers everywhere have been encouraged to take up boro cultivation, so although one fifth of the thanas have less than 1 per cent, another fifth have only 1 per cent of the T.C.A. under boro, and the middle quintile 2–4 per cent. The uppermost quintile extends from 13 per cent to include three thanas with 94, 92 and 87 per cent respectively. There is a continuous region of thanas in the top quintile through the Meghna Depression into northern Comilla, and smaller groups of high percentage thanas in south Dacca and Rajshahi, related probably to deep depressions (of partly tectonic origin), and in central and southern Chittagong District.

The Fishing Industry

Fishing represents the livelihood of upwards of five million Bangalees, most of them Hindus and most of them very poor. Ninety per cent of fish production is from inland fisheries, and it is a sad fact that this major source of animal protein for a protein-starved population operates under increasing difficulty as agriculture becomes more efficiently organised. Pressure to increase agricultural production, especially of paddy, leads to the reduction by drainage of the area of lakes and swamps which traditionally have been used for fishing. Chemical control of plant pests, diseases and weeds threatens increasingly to pollute fishing areas.

Yet the potential demand for fish in Bangladesh and the nearby conurbations of West Bengal is enormous, and the theoretical capacity of the country to become a region of intensive fish culture is very considerable. The lowlands abound with great and small rivers and natural and man-made ponds. The seaward portion of the delta, particularly in the Sundarbans, and the adjoining estuaries and the Bay of Bengal are already rich fishing grounds. Unfortunately the generally backward state of overland communications, and the technologically unsophisticated methods of handling the catch, hamper the development of an industry dealing with a commodity notoriously perishable in the humid tropics. Freezing plants at Khulna and Chittagong process prawns, but by and large preservation of the catch is limited to sun-drying on beaches or river banks during the dry season, or the ingenious though laborious system of shipping fish alive in the holds of country boats, awash to the gunwales and equipped with traditional waterscoops to keep them afloat.

Apart from some efforts to establish co-operative marine fishing enterprises, out of Chittagong for example, the fishing industry awaits effective development. Before this can occur, government authorities will have to take steps to resolve the conflicts of interest that set farmer against fisherman, by encouraging where possible the profitable combination of their respective activities in the same area. A first step could be the restoration and development of the innumerable excavated tanks, many of which were traditionally sources of fish for the largely vegetarian Hindu landlords who controlled much of the fishing industry prior to partition. In 1960 about one farm in sixteen reported having fish ponds, the total area of which amounted to 42,500 ha (172,000 acres) but the total area of excavated tanks was about three times as great, most of which could be used for fish culture.

CHAPTER SIX

AGRICULTURAL REGIONS

A first approach to combining the evidence of the crop patterns discussed above into a scheme of regions is Fig. 6.1 which maps the principal crop associations based on the rice crops. Each of the four rice crops is sufficiently dominant over the next most important crop in some areas as to constitute a monoculture. Thus transplanted aman is monocultural in the Barind and the Saline Tidal Delta, broadcast aman in the central belt of depressions from Chalan Bil to the lower Meghna, boro paddy in the Meghna Depression and aus (though less clearly dominant) in the northeast of the Moribund Delta.

Combinations of transplanted aman with aus (generally with the former dominant, as would be expected from its premier status among rice crops) are widespread in the North Bengal Sandy Alluvial Fan, the plain of the Old Brahmaputra, the hill-foot plains in southern Sylhet, the Tippera Surface, north Chittagong and the Non-Saline Tidal Delta. These areas have in common only shallow to moderate flooding. Broadcast aman combines with aus in more

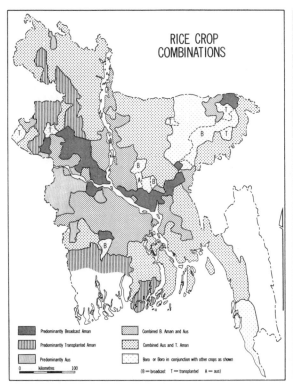

FIG. 6.1   Area differences in combinations of rice crops by thanas.

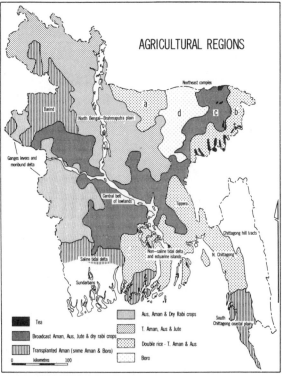

FIG. 6.2   Agricultural regions.

deeply flooding areas as along the Brahmaputra–Jamuna banks, Faridpur and adjacent areas to the west in the lower parts of the Moribund Delta, and to the east on the fringe of the Tippera Surface. Broadcast aman is in combination with boro in a belt in mid Sylhet, but other associations involving boro are found in nine scattered patches of limited extent.

Further simplification of the pattern of agricultural activity is made in Fig. 6.2, which may be summarised thus:

1. The Barind: near monoculture of transplanted aman. Some diversity occurs along the Atrai terraces, and two low-lying thanas with boro as an associated crop may also be linked with the Barind.
2. North Bengal–Brahmaputra Plain, including the North Bengal Sandy Alluvial Fan, the stabilised flood plains of the Tista and Old Brahmaputra, the Brahmaputra–Jamuna active flood plain and the Madhupur Tract: transplanted aman and aus vie for primacy in a consistent combination, which generally includes jute.
3. The Central Belt of Lowlands links the Atrai–Chalan Bil depression, the Dhaleswari depression in South Dacca, Lower Meghna, Faridpur Bil and the floodlands of the Padma: broadcast aman, sometimes monocultural, often in association with aus, and sometimes with jute also, and dry rabi crops.
4. The Moribund Delta and adjacent Ganges levees: Aus, widely with broadcast and less commonly transplanted aman, and with significantly high percentages of dry rabi crops.
5. The Saline Tidal Delta: approaching absolute monoculture of transplanted aman.
6. The southeast region of double rice cropping with transplanted aman and aus: the Non-Saline Tidal Delta, the Estuarine Islands, the charlands of Noakhali and the Tippera–North Chittagong Plain. Aus is generally secondary in importance to transplanted aman. Jute is insignificant nor does the dry rabi crop group feature prominently. Boro is of growing importance in Chittagong parcularly, but of small significance in the Tidal Delta and Estuary.

7. South Chittagong Coastal Plain: transplanted aman and in areas not affected by tides, boro paddy and dry rabi crops as fairly modest associations.
8. The northeast region lying between the Old Brahmaputra and the foot-hill edge that marks the borders with India: this is a complex of sub-regions, forming an irregular saucer-like basin unified by a common drainage outlet, the Meghna at Bhairab Bazar.

   (a) North of Mymensingh and west of the Someswari the western rim of the basin is an area of transplanted aman with aus which might alternatively be regarded as part of region (2), above. However, its drainage east via the Kangsa to the centre of the Meghna Depression is independent of the Brahmaputra.
   (b) Skirting the hill country in South Sylhet the edge of the basin is a similar region of transplanted aman with aus, characterised on its hill margin by tea gardens established on benchlands above the several lakes which fluctuate in size according to season.
   (c) A slightly lower plain adjoins this piedmont, extending from the foot of the Shillong Plateau north of Sylhet Town, to the southern extremity of Sylhet District. Here floods spread early in the rains but not generally to excessive depth. Broadcast aman is followed by boro, utilising the abundant standing water remaining in the dry season.
   (d) At the heart of the Meghna Depression deep extensive flooding persists through the rainy season, and very little land can be cropped at all until the dry season. Boro paddy is then cultivated as a transplanted irrigated crop and attains near monocultural status. Much of the region's cultivation is done by migrants who come from neighbouring districts by boat to grow boro and graze their cattle on the lush pastures.

9. The Chittagong Hill Tracts: aus, with some transplanted aman and boro on the valley floors, shifting cultivation (jhum) on the slopes. (See below and Fig. 6.3.)

SHIFTING CULTIVATION

The people of the Chittagong Hill Tracts, although possessed of a culture very different from that of the plains folk, have added permanent field cultivation in the Bangalee style to their traditional swidden or jhum agriculture. Jhum cultivation involves clearing slopes covered in a three- or four-year growth of bamboo, burning the dried rubbish and planting mixed crops of upland rice, maize, millets, sesamum, cotton, bananas and vegetables such as beans, cucumbers and gourds. Clearing takes place during the dry season, and burning in March, when the hill country becomes shrouded in a haze of blue smoke. With the first of the 'little rains' planting begins, and continues into May. The *dao*, a broad-bladed knife, is used both to slash the bamboo and as a dibble to make the hole in which the mixed seeds are sown or the banana cuttings planted.

Weeds are a major problem for the jhum cultivator through the months of June and July until the crop plants are tall enough to shade them out. Wild pigs, barking deer and birds can cause havoc to the jhum patches far from the permanent settlements, so it is customary for the cultivator to stay on his plot in a temporary hut while the crops are maturing. Being a mixture of crops, harvest is a continuing activity from July when the first vegetables are ready. Some early rice may be cut in August along with sesamum (an oilseed), but the main harvest of both crops is in September–October when the rains are slackening. Cotton then remains to be picked in November–December after which the land is allowed to revert to bamboo jungle, though the bananas will continue to be picked for a while. After three years or so the cycle of cultivation can be repeated.

Jhum land is not owned by the individual who cultivates it, but rather by the tribal village community whose headman is responsible for distributing the land among applicants who pay a capitation fee for the privilege of jhuming. It is generally the younger families in the tribe who practise jhum

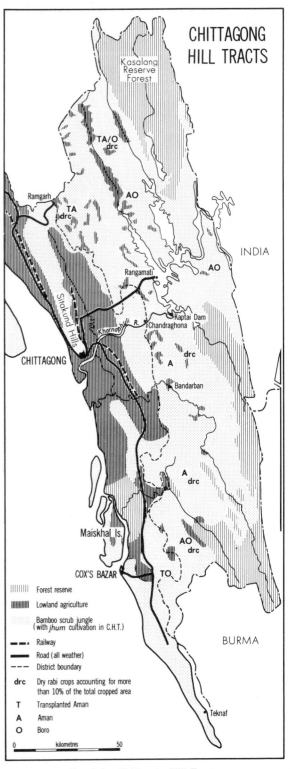

FIG. 6.3   Chittagong Hill Tracts.

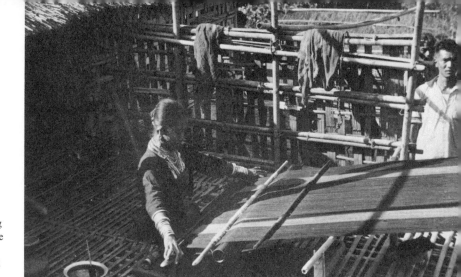

21. A Tipra tribeswoman hand-weaving a skirt length on the verandah of her home in the Chittagong Hill Tracts. The fine bamboo structure of the house, floors and walls can be seen.

22. Tenchaungya tribal house built on piles, near Rangamati, Chittagong Hill Tracts. Womenfolk weaving skirts from jhum-grown cotton on hand looms while baby plays with the goat kid. Firewood bundles in the left foreground.

23. Recently abandoned jhum clearing with temporary hut in Chittagong Hill Tracts.

24. Magh houses and the Chief's local transport. Chittagong Hill Tracts.

25. Elephant working teak logs. Chittagong Hill Tracts near Chandraghona.

26. Chittagong Hill Tracts near Rangamati. Dissected Tertiary sandstones and shales. The near slopes carry mixed crops of upland rice, millets, beans, cotton, etc., planted by shifting (jhum) cultivators. A patch of bananas can be seen near the bamboo hut. The hillsides are cleared of bamboo and scrub in rotation every three or four years. The valley floors are under permanent cultivation for paddy: a farmer is seen pulling seedling rice for transplantation.

27. Kaptai Lake near the Hydroelectric station. Country boat being lifted out of the dam to be transferred to the Karnaphuli River about 50 metres lower. Bamboo bundles and other craft await their turn.

28. Magh houses at Bandarban, Chittagong Hill Tracts: pigs and poultry scavenge beneath the buildings.

29. Mro houses, Chittagong Hill Tracts: this tribe depends entirely on shifting cultivation.

cultivation before inheriting ownership of permanent fields later in life, but there are tribes in the
more rugged parts of the hills, such as the Mro, who
have little land other than jhum.

Along the valley bottoms a narrow strip of paddy
land is cleared, and can readily be provided with
irrigation from the small streams. Such land generally carries broadcast aus paddy, but transplanted
aman may also be grown. In the dry season light
lands traditionally have a rabi crop of mustard,
tobacco or vegetables, and the lower paddy lands
are now being brought under boro. 'Dry' rabi crops
occupy over 10 per cent of the total crop area in
most thanas.

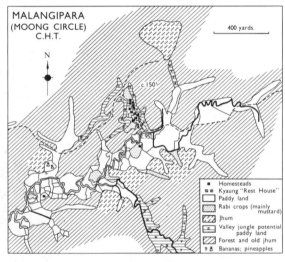

FIG. 6.4   Malangipara: a typical village of shifting and permanent cultivators in the northern part of the Chittagong Hill
Tracts. Note the scale line 400 yards is 366 metres, and the
altitudes shown are c.150 ft (46 m) and 95 ft (29 m) above sea
level.

Figure 6.4 of Malangipara village shows land use
in a typical area in the northern part of the
Chittagong Hill Tracts. The total tribal population
supported by this mixed shifting and permanent
cultivation numbers about 360,000, mostly
Chakma, Maghs, Tipra and Tenchungya. It is a
population now facing considerable difficulties. The
Hill Tracts contain the only sites for hydroelectric
power development in Bangladesh, and are also the
principal source of hardwoods, including teak and
garjan. The establishment of the Kaptai Power
Station on the Karnaphuli created a lake which
flooded the valley lands of about 90,000 tribal

people. This put increased pressure on the remaining
areas available for jhum clearing outside the catchment of the dam, and no thoroughly satisfactory
answer has been found for resettling the displaced
tribesmen. Intensive horticulture may be a part
solution for some, for they have a tradition of good
husbandry on permanent village gardens of spices,
such as ginger and turmeric, and vegetables and a
liking for rearing pigs and chickens.

PLANTATION AGRICULTURE

Tea planting was begun in the 1870s when British
(largely Scottish) entrepreneurs established gardens
using labour brought in from Orissa and West
Bengal. The descendants of this labour force still
work the plantations, picking being done by
women, and other tasks by the men. The local
Bangalee Muslim has as yet shown little liking for
the idea of his womenfolk working in public, and
the job is left in the hands of a Hindu minority
group. Management has however been taken over
progressively by non-Europeans.

About 43,000 ha (106,000 acres) are under tea
in 147 gardens, mostly in Sylhet, with a few in
Chittagong, the Hill Tracts and Comilla. Small experimental acres are under coffee and rubber. While
the best estates in the Bangladesh tea industry were
among the most efficient in the world in terms of
yield per acre, ageing of the gardens and the failure
to replant and to modernise has been harmful to the
industry's economic position. Until 1965 tea was a
valuable export from the then undivided Pakistan,
but increased internal demand kept all production
for home consumption. Bangladesh's independence
means a sudden loss of the West Pakistan market
and the problem of disposing of more than half the
potential crop of about 32 million kg (70 million
pounds). Unfortunately in terms of cost efficiency
Bangladesh is in a poor competitive position on the
world market.

The tea produced is 'lowland tea' suitable for
bulking by overseas blenders with more flavoured
leaf from elsewhere. The gardens produce heavily
for nine months of the year, January to April being
a period of shut-down of the tea factories and of
pruning and maintenance of the gardens. The ces-
sation of the rains is the principal cause of stoppage,
and there are prospects of setting up spray irrigated

30. Mro woman and child ginning cotton on the verandah of their bamboo home in the Chittagong Hill Tracts. Note carrying baskets and cooking pots behind. The woman has large silver ear-rings, beads and bangles, and a diminutive homewoven skirt.

31. Pruning tea bushes, Sylhet District. This operation is carried out during the short dry season when growth of young shoots is minimal and so picking has ceased. The wide branching trees are a planted cover to reduce direct sunlight. The women are Oriyas, third generation descendants of migrants into Sylhet from Orissa, brought in to establish the tea industry in an area where the local Moslem women do not generally work in the open away from home.

gardens in future, and so increasing the efficiency of operation of the estates. The most urgent need is systematically to replant old tea with high-yielding bushes, but capital costs are very high, and the expatriate sector is naturally reluctant to invest money until the politicians have guaranteed the industry security of tenure of their gardens, and the export prospects become clearer.

The possibility of substituting home-grown rubber for imports has prompted experimental planting in southern Chittagong where temperature and rainfall conditions approach most nearly those of the natural rubber producing countries — most of them near-equatorial in location. A major drawback is said to be the proneness of the coastal regions to cyclones which could uproot rubber trees on plantations and might render the enterprise uneconomic. Coffee planting could suffer similarly, but might succeed in Sylhet where cyclones do not penetrate.

CHAPTER SEVEN

AGRICULTURAL CHANGE

The Bangalee farmer is characteristically a small-scale entrepreneur, achieving a very low return for the minimal amount of capital and the long hours of labour he and his family invest. To bring his standard of living above its present bare subsistence level requires at the very least that his working capital and the efficiency of his farming operations be increased and so the return to the total family investment. He has to be educated towards a scientific approach to farming, so that he can adapt to his particular situation whatever modern knowledge and knowhow is applicable.

Traditionally much of his land has lain fallow through the dry season or has carried a low-yielding rabi crop. If he has a source of water available he has used the technique of irrigation known to him to grow boro paddy, raising the water by wearisome human effort. Only in the hills can farmers train the natural flow of streams to water their fields. Government at one level or another has recognised the farmer's situation as being capable of change by methods beyond his means as a private individual. In the tradition of government departments large-scale projects have been undertaken to divert rivers into channels by gravity or power pumping and to bring about conventional canal irrigation. There is however only limited scope in Bangladesh for irrigation by gravity canal. The nature of the terrain and the widely dispersed resources of water in the dry season call for a dispersed system of water delivery units such as small capacity low lift pumps drawing on surface water, and tubewells. Initially government has to provide pumps and wells and help farmers organise themselves effectively to use them, but much initiative remains at the village level.

At other times of the year it is superfluity of water that bedevils the farmer, drowning his crops

and deterring him from investing capital and effort in the face of the risk of loss. Here Government necessarily plays the major role in surveying the extent and origin of floods and in designing and executing the flood protection works. Guaranteed some known level of protection against the hazard, the individual farmer can replan his enterprise to take advantage of the new conditions in his environment.

The provision of a guaranteed supply of water in the dry season and the assurance of flood protection in the rains are preconditions to increasing productivity on the farm in many areas, but do not of themselves ensure optimum levels of yield per hectare or output per man. These can only be achieved by changing the nature of the inputs at the farm level, changes that require a conscious commitment on the part of the cultivator to an improved system of farming. The technological changes that have had greatest impact in recent years are the introduction of high-yielding varieties of rice, the extended use of irrigation principally through low-lift pumps, and the use of fertilisers. Improvements in the control of pests, diseases and weeds have also been initiated. Obviously these several changes are in considerable degree interdependent. There is no use changing to H.Y.V. of boro paddy if water or the essential fertilisers are not going to be available.

While the distribution of pumps for dry season cropping had been progressing for a decade, the real impetus to modernisation (using this word to encompass the acceptance by the farmer of the need for the whole gamut of technological changes) seems to have come in the wake of the 'green revolution'. The promise of much enhanced yields of rice at a period when demand was strong and prices buoyant must have persuaded many sceptics of earlier attempts by the agricultural extension services to encourage new techniques, to decide to apply the full package of new inputs. The situation now is that the farmers through their co-operatives or local agricultural officers are calling for the new inputs at a rate the administrative machinery is hard pressed to meet.

RICE PRODUCTION

It is perhaps easy to be carried away by all the publicity that has surrounded the green revolution since about 1968 into imagining that all increases in rice production are attributable to it and that its effects have penetrated everywhere. A brief review of rice production in Bangladesh since the partition of India in 1947 will show how acreage and total output have increased over the years before the new

H.Y.V. rices were available, and will place in perspective the very recent, remarkable but still relatively small advances of the years since their introduction. The green revolution, while it is certainly under way in Bangladesh, is so far a demonstration of potential rather than an actuality of general achievement.

Figure 7.1 shows the upward trend in total rice area and production since 1947. Area has risen from a mean of 7·9 million ha (19·5 million acres) in the late 1940s to a range of 7·9 to 8·9 million ha (19·5 to 22 million acres) through the 1950s, 8·5 to 10·4 million ha (21 to 25·6 million acres) in the 1960s, culminating in figures over 9·7 million ha (24 million acres) since 1967–68. In Fig. 7.2 these areas are broken down among the three main seasonal rice crops, aman, aus and boro. The major crop, aman, shows least change, but it is note-

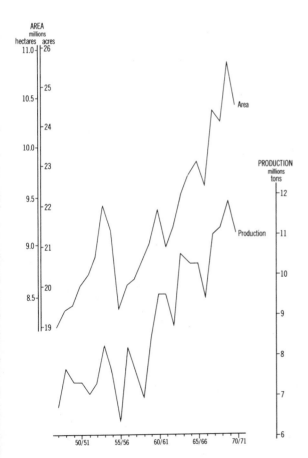

Fig. 7.1   Rice: total area and production in long tons, 1947–71.

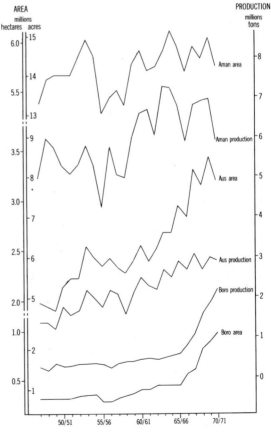

Fig. 7.2   Rice: Aman, aus and boro area and production, 1947–71. Note that the area scale is discontinuous.

worthy that having fluctuated in the 1950s within the range 4·9 to 6·0 million ha (13 to 14·9 million acres) with four years below 5·7 million ha (14 million acres), it has achieved a steadier higher level through the 1960s, consistently better than 5·7 million ha (14·1 million acres).

The aus area shows a more vigorous upward trend from a mean of about 2·1 million ha (5·1 million acres) in 1950–51 to 2·4 million ha (6 million acres) around 1960–61 and 3·2 million ha (7·9 million acres) over the quinquennium ending 1970–71. A possible explanation for the greater actual (and proportional) rise of aus acreage is that in response to population pressure it was easier to expand aus cultivation than to find space for more aman, already in occupation of a much larger part of the cultivable area.

The area under boro shows an even more dramatic rise, in this case almost certainly in response to technological change as small capacity pumps came into use. From a consistent level around 324,000 ha (800,000 acres) through the 1950s it mounted to 440,000 ha (1·1 million acres) in the early 1960s before 'taking off' after 1965–66 to climb to almost 1 million ha (2·4 million acres) by 1970–71 and an anticipated 1·1 million ha (2·7 million acres) by 1973–74.

Thus in an overall expansion of the rice area amounting to over 2·4 million ha (6 million acres), since 1947, aus accounts for 1·2 million ha (3 million acres) and boro for about 784,000 ha (1·9 million acres).

The production curves of aman and aus march in step with area, reflecting year to year variations due to drought or flood, and a general rise in response to the population's demand. Population increased 21 per cent between 1951–61 but total rice production lagged behind. Boro production shows a different pattern. Since it is almost invariably irrigated,

the first high-yielding variety IR-8 was taken up by boro cultivators with an immediate impact upon yields which had already begun to rise with the widespread use of pump irrigation in the late 1960s (Fig. 7.3). From a few hundred in the late 1950s pumps numbered over 24,000 in 1970–71 and by 1973 may have reached 35,000.

The patterns of change in yields are shown in Table 7.1.

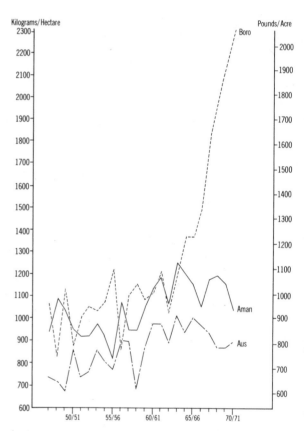

FIG. 7.3   Yields in kilograms per hectare and pounds per acre of aman, aus and boro paddy, 1947–71.

TABLE 7.1
Average yields of rice
(kg per hectare and pounds per acre)

	Aman		Aus		Boro	
	kg/ha	lb/acre	kg/ha	lb/acre	kg/ha	lb/acre
1947–50	1023	913	709	633	1005	897
1950–55	940	839	802	716	1014	905
1955–60	977	872	829	740	1088	971
1960–65	1189	1061	968	864	1208	1078
1965–70	1152	1028	922	823	1752	1563

(Note, in 1969–70 the average yield for transplanted aman was 1854 kg per ha (1654 lb per acre) and for broadcast aman 1576 kg per ha (1406 lb per acre).)

The quinquennial averages fail to do justice to the meteoric rise of boro yields, indicated on the graph, to 2306 kg per hectare (2057 lb per acre) by 1970–71. IR-8 has been increasingly used since 1967–68 and by 1971–72 56 per cent of the boro crop was represented by the improved varieties. The overall boro yield was 1996 kg per ha (1781 lb per acre) and that of the H.Y.V., 3050 kg per ha (2721 lb per acre).

The New Rice Varieties

The fundamental objective of research at the International Rice Research Institute, at Los Baños in the Philippines, has been, and continues to be, to discover and to breed varieties of rice which are adapted to the conditions found in the rice-growing tropical countries of South and Southeast Asia and which respond to fertilisers. The first variety to be released for general use was IR-8, which has found favour as a boro type in Bangladesh. Among the characteristics possessed by IR-8 and to a degree by other high-yield varieties from the I.R.R.I. are:

1. shortness of stem to give strength and prevent the crop lodging or flattening when the head is formed; however, shortness is a disadvantage in areas subject to flood;
2. lack of sensitivity to photo-period. Many varieties, such as those grown in the aman season, only flower if the days are shortening. Such rices cannot be grown as dry season crops as they would come to maturity as days are lengthening;
3. responsiveness to nitrogenous fertiliser. The crop needs to be well irrigated to make use of the nitrogen applied;
4. relatively short growing season to enable more than one rice crop to be taken during the year.

It follows that the basic needs of IR-8 are a closely controlled water supply and nitrogenous fertiliser. In addition, protection against fungus diseases and insects may be necessary if the crop is grown in warm humid conditions. In Bangladesh in winter the clear sunny days are ideal for IR-8 from this point of view, but the variety is rather sensitive to cold, which delays it maturing, increasing to 170 days the period from December sowing to harvest. Such a delay may interfere with the cultivation of the aus crop that might follow on the same land.

An alternative to IR-8 for cool season use is the dwarf variety Chandina, IR-532, similarly non-sensitive to photo-period, but having better resistance to cold as well as to pests and diseases. It matures a month sooner than IR-8. The local boro varieties are relatively short season types but tend to respond to fertiliser by growing too tall and lodging badly.

32. 'Ammunition' for the green revolution: sacks of potash and superphosphate fertilizer on the Karnaphuli bank.

Yet a third new variety, Mala, IR-272, which grows 1·2 m (*c.* 4 ft) tall, may be used as a boro crop in low-lying land where there is an early risk of flooding, though it is more specifically an aus type. In the cool season it needs 150 days; as an aus crop only 110 days.

During the hotter and more humid seasons when aus and aman are traditionally grown a different and more difficult set of problems faces the plant breeder. The contrast between the crops with regard to photosensitivity is made use of by the farmer who broadcasts mixed aus and aman, harvesting the first before the second has responded to the reducing day length of July and later. Sensitivity to photo-period can be an advantage. Without it a short season variety planted say in early June might come to maturity in August when floodwaters were still too deep to allow harvesting. A photosensitive type would not mature for at least another month. Most aman rices are well adapted to growing in floodwaters more than a metre deep, and cannot on many sites be replaced by shortstemmed varieties. Aus and aman rices need to be resistant to diseases and insect pests.

The prospects for using I.R.R.I. high-yielding varieties in the rainy season are best in the case of (*a*) aus, traditionally a fairly shortstemmed rice that cannot tolerate flooding; however aus is usually broadcast and rainfed, not irrigated; and (*b*) aman grown on land which floods only shallowly.

The most successful new rice in the aman season is IR-20, a short season (120–135 day) variety, shortstemmed, disease resistant, slightly photoperiod sensitive and of good eating quality: altogether a highly satisfactory rice. By 1971–72 IR-20 occupied 253,000 ha (625,500 acres), 14 per cent of the transplanted aman area. Perhaps as much as 4·0 million ha (10 million acres) of land which floods normally to a depth of no more than one metre could carry IR-20 – effectively the whole of the transplanted aman area.

For deeper water a new rice, IR-442, shows promise with a potential to stand in 1·5 m (5 ft) of floodwater, but a preference for not more than 1 m (3 ft). IR-442 illustrates well one problem of adapting new varieties to the flood areas of Bangladesh. It matures in 137–145 days, but not being photoperiod sensitive it will develop strictly by time. If it is planted early it may ripen too soon and be ready to harvest before floods have receded. Planting later in July leads to maturing in November when cool weather will result in lower than optimal yields.

The diagram in Fig. 7.4 sets out the cropping calendar for the new varieties and points up some environmental limitations. Although the introduction of several high-yielding varieties will in the short run give the country a chance to achieve self-sufficiency, the longer term prospects for increasing rice production in Bangladesh are subject to a number of constraints. Water resources in the dry season may permit the cultivation of about 1·2 million ha (3 million acres) of boro paddy provided pumps and tubewells are installed. It may prove a more productive use of part of these resources to concentrate them on ensuring a more extensive early aus crop which can come to maturity on the basis of rainfall in May–June and be followed on the same land by an aman crop.

Diffusion of H.Y.V.

Knowledge and subsequent adoption of an innovation, such as a new rice variety of exceptional yield potential, take time to spread. In the case of the high-yielding rices the farmer has not only to hear of the innovation but must also be in a position to obtain supplies of seed and essential inputs like fertiliser, and must assure himself of an irrigation water supply if necessary. Seed and fertiliser in Bangladesh will normally be obtained through the government agricultural agencies. The provision of irrigation water may necessitate the farmers in a village agreeing to co-operate to make channels to their fields and to request a pump from the authorities.

The first H.Y.V. to be distributed in Bangladesh was IR-8, which was suitable as a boro paddy. By 1968–69, 18 per cent of the boro crop was under IR-8 and other dwarf varieties, and this percentage rose to 27 (235,000 ha (580,000 acres)), 35 (347,000 ha (857,000 acres)) and 36 per cent (322,000 ha (795,000 acres)) in the years that followed. But for the disturbances through 1971 the increase would probably have been even greater. On the aman crop the impact of H.Y.V. came later, with IR-20, and has affected only areas of shallow flooding. Even so the area planted to H.Y.V. rose from 12,000 ha (29,200 acres) in 1969–70 to 81,000 ha (199,800 acres) and 254,000 ha

Crop calendar for high-yielding rices
(growing periods in days)

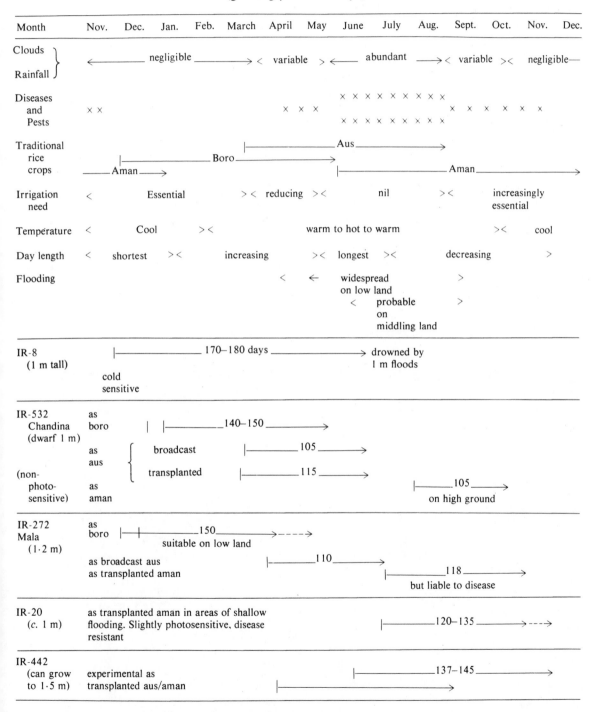

(625,600 acres) in 1970–71 and 1971–72. By the latter year 4·7 per cent of all aman, and 7 per cent of transplanted aman was H.Y.V. Aus, since it is mainly broadcast and difficult to irrigate reliably, shows the lowest percentage of adoption of H.Y.V., only 1·6 per cent being achieved by 1971–72.

Figure 7.5 maps some significant data on these developments. It is clear that in the traditional boro-growing regions the proportion of H.Y.V. is relatively low. The Meghna Depression in Sylhet and the Kishoreganj subdivision of east Mymensingh each show a smaller area under H.Y.V. than several districts where boro is more of an innovation. It would be interesting to know why this is so. One possible explanation is that, as many of the boro cultivators migrate to the remote heart of the Meghna Depression for the boro season only, they are not as adequately served by extension services through which information and material inputs generally flow.

CONTROLLING THE CULTIVATORS' PHYSICAL ENVIRONMENT

The past and continuing efforts by government agencies to assist the farmer by intervening in the natural environment may be stated as being projects

(a) to redistribute available surface water;
(b) to exploit groundwater resources;
(c) to protect cultivated land from floods;
(d) to prevent the ingress of saline water.

Surface water
It is of vital interest for Bangladesh to utilise its main resource – land – to the utmost. In order to do this, as much land as possible has to be under productive use at all times. With only 25 per cent cultivated during the dry season and 47 per cent during the bhadoi season there remains considerable scope for increasing the total cropped area, *if water can be made available.* By reducing the growing period the breeding of fast maturing H.Y.V. rices much improves the

33.   Low lift pump irrigating transplanted paddy.

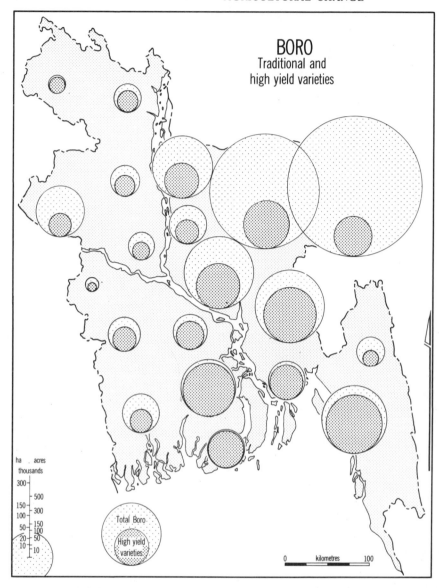

BORO
Traditional and
high yield varieties

ha   acres
thousands
300—
      ⌐ 500
150— ⌐ 300
100—
 50— ⌐ 150
      ⌐ 100
 20— ⌐ 50
 10— ⌐ 10

Total Boro

High yield
varieties

0   kilometres   100

FIG. 7.5   Boro paddy:
area under traditional and
H.Y. Varieties by districts.

prospect of multiple cropping, but puts greater demands on water resources for crops grown out of the rainy season.

Impressive advances have been made in dry season irrigation of rice since low-lift power-driven pumps were introduced. The areal distribution of some 24,000 pumps in 1971–72 is mapped in Fig. 7.6. Theoretically the standard 2-cusec pump can command 35 ha (100 acres) of rice, and it would thus require 30,000 pumps to serve the 1·2 million ha (3 million acres) which it is considered feasible to irrigate in this manner. For a variety of reasons, including problems of mechanical maintenance in a country where engineering skills are in short supply, and a reluctance to run pumps at night when water might escape through unnoticed breaks in channels, it is more realistic to estimate that 45,000–55,000 pumps might be needed. Water to irrigate a further 2·8 million ha (7 million acres) is estimated to be available in the river systems of the country but would have to be directed into areas where it could be used.

The only major diversion of water undertaken to date is in the Ganges–Kobadak Scheme which draws heavily on the Ganges at Bheramara to irrigate a projected 89,000 ha (220,000 acres (net))

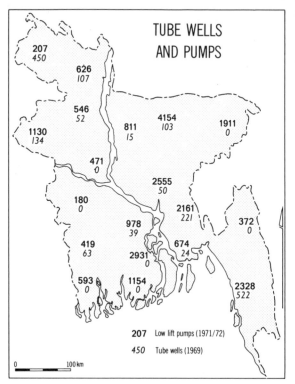

FIG. 7.6   Tubewells and low-lift pumps by districts. (Note that the figure of 522 tubewells in Chittagong District is not reliable.)

FIG. 7.7   Ganges–Kobadak Scheme: Phase I. The main canals follow the highest land, i.e. the river levees, from which secondary channels can command the lower ground away from the river.

in Kushtia District (Fig. 7.7). Technical problems have bedevilled the project since its inception in the 1950s. In concept the scheme proposes pumping Ganges water into a canal system which would command areas of the Moribund Delta where a perennial supply of nutrient-rich Ganges water would upgrade the region's agricultural activity. A further objective is to bring fresh water to the Saline Tidal Delta in Khulna, which has deteriorated agriculturally with the decay of the Ganges distributaries allowing salt water to penetrate further inland, so restricting cropping effectively to a single aman planting. Poldering of the saline-affected area and the supply of fresh water could reverse the present wasting of these lands. It now seems unlikely that the low-level flow of the Ganges when India completes the Farakka Barrage to divert water to keep clear the Hooghly at Calcutta, will allow the earlier targets of the Ganges–Kobadak Scheme to be achieved. The irrigation of polders in the Saline Delta will now depend on the prospects of diverting Brahmaputra–Jamuna water into the Garai and thence into Khulna.

The present status of the G–K Project is that of 49,000 ha (120,000 acres) commanded in Kushtia Phase I a net area of 35,000 ha (85,400 acres) was irrigated in 1969–70. Unreliability of supply due to breakdowns in the 10,000 kW power station and pump units has no doubt discouraged farmers, but the overall design of gravity canals and feeders at

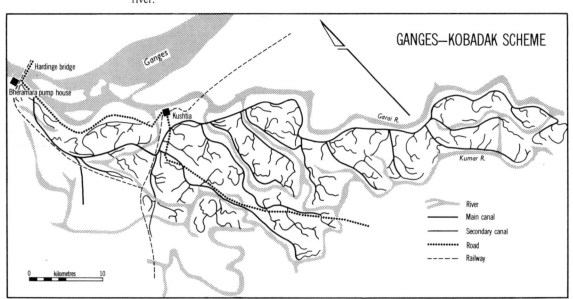

34. Ganges–Kobadak Project Pump houses, lifting water into Kushtia canal at Bheramara. (See Fig. 7.7.)

best delivers too little water to the more remote cultivators continuing to farm fragmented holdings.

The changes in the cropping pattern of the Kushtia Phase I area are summarised in Table 7.2. The most important impact of the scheme has been in promoting transplanted aman through guaranteeing irrigation to supplement rainfall. Dry season cropping has changed very little, and the bhadoi season total area has actually decreased slightly. However, yields have responded well to the

TABLE 7.2
Area of crops, Kushtia, Phase I

	Pre-project ha ('000)	Pre-project acres ('000)	1969–70 ha ('000)	1969–70 acres ('000)	Pre-project yields mds/acre kg/ha	Pre-project yields mds/acre lb/acre	1969–70 yields kg/ha	1969–70 yields lb/acre
Bhadoi crops								
Broadcast aus	16	40	16	39	1106	987	2400	2140
Transplanted aus			1·2	3			2580/4150*	2300/3700*
Mixed aus–aman	13	32	8	20			1530	1370
Jute	8	20	9	22				
Others			1·2	3				
	37	92	35	87				
Aman crops								
Broadcast aman	9	23	8	19	1106	987	2030	1810
Transplanted aman			12	29			2950/4430*	2630/3950*
Others (incl. some aman)			4	10				
	9	23	24	58				
Rabi crops and others								
Boro			0·1	0·2			2950/5070*	2630/4530*
Wheat	2·4	6	4	9	461	412	1570/2120*	1400/1890*
Pulses	12	29	15	36				
Sugar cane	1·6	4	1·6	4				
Others	4·5	11	1·6	4				
	20·5	51	22	53				
Cropping intensity	138%		192%					

* H.Y.V.

greater reliability of water supply, though so far the advantages of transplanted varieties over broadcast rice seem hardly to have been exploited in the *bhadoi* season. Indications are that the introduction of H.Y.V. will increase the proportion of transplanted aus.

Groundwater

Proposals to harness the unruly Tista by a barrage located near the point where the river enters Bangladesh and to irrigate 324,000 ha (800,000 acres) mostly in Rangpur and Bogra have been dropped in recent years. The Tista's violence in flood and difficulties in finding sites for a secure dam were among the reasons for abandoning the scheme, and the recent development of groundwater resources beneath the North Bengal Sandy Alluvial Fan has made it a less attractive proposition. The relatively coarse alluvium of the fan facilitates the recharge of aquifers lying no great depth below the surface, though the same factor means that the region's soils tend to be permeable and thirsty, not retentive of irrigation or rainwater. Figure 7.6 shows the distribution of agricultural tubewells by districts, and clearly indicates the concentration in the northwest, where in the Thakurgaon Project alone some 25,000 ha (62,000 acres) are irrigated (out of a Bangladesh total of about 47,000 ha (116,000 acres)). Here wells are sited about half a mile apart and many are powered by electrical pumps of about 3-cusec capacity driven from the power grid. Water is led to the fields in cement-lined channels to reduce wastage by seepage. There are also diesel-driven wells of smaller capacity. Compared with low-lift pumps, tubewells represent as much as eight times the capital investment per acre commanded, but they have the advantage of greater reliability of supply towards the end of the dry season. Data comparing agricultural activity before and after the installation of tubewells in Thakurgaon are shown in Table 7.3.

The Dinajpur District had among the lowest cropping intensities in the country, and it is something of a miracle that the tubewell areas now carry

TABLE 7.3
Crop areas Thakurgaon Tubewell Project

	Pre-project ha ('000)	Pre-project acres ('000)	1969–70 ha ('000)	1969–70 acres ('000)	Pre-project yields kg/ha	Pre-project yields lb/acre	1969–70 yields kg/ha	1969–70 yields lb/acre
Bhadoi crops								
Broadcast aus	3	7	9	23	922	823	1,937	1,728
Transplanted aus	0·02	0·04	6	16	1,291	1,152	2,766/5,072*	2,468/4,525*
Jute	0·4	1	1	3	1,199	1,070	1,291	1,152
Others			3	7				
	4	9	19	49				
Aman crops								
Broadcast aman	1·6	4	0·4	1	922	823	1,937	1,728
Transplanted aman	21	52	23	58	1,106	987	2,766	2,468
Others			0·8	2				
	23	56	24	61				
Rabi crops and others								
Boro	0·1	0·3	0·4	1	1,745	1,316	3,228/5,072*	2,880/4,525*
Wheat	0·04	0·1	1	3	554	494	1,383/3,228*	1,234/2,880*
Mustard	0·8	2	2	4	323	288	646	576
Sugar cane	2	6	1	3	27,667	24,684	50,815	45,336
Others	1	3	2	5				
	4	11	6	16				
Total all crops	31	76	49	126				
Cropping intensity		109%		192%				

* H.Y.V.

35. Drilling a tubewell near Feni, Noakhali District. The datepalm on the left has been notched to extract the sugary sap.

36. Lined channel of tubewell irrigation project Thakurgaon, Dinajpur District. Minor distributary in foreground.

two crops per year on almost all the area commanded. The bhadoi crop show the most remarkable increase. Thakurgaon has a long dry season, and a relatively late start to the rains, which in combination with droughty soils makes rain-fed cultivation hazardous in the pre-monsoon period. Tubewells have introduced a radical new element into the farmers' experience at a scale of operation and management more likely to win their co-operation than the monolithic canal irrigation system such as the Ganges–Kobadak. Figure 7.8 shows a typical tubewell scheme layout.

Groundwater reserves underlie most of the lowlands of Bangladesh, but are largely unsurveyed. In the Tidal Delta salinity of groundwater is only to be expected, but elsewhere there is considerable agricultural advantage to be gained from drilling tubewells. The Barind promises well in this respect, since tubewell irrigation could support a boro or early aus crop where at present only aman is possible. Groundwater conditions are likely to be specially good along the hill margins in the east. Apart from supporting irrigated paddy, which is very demanding of water, tubewells can help the cultivator diversify dry season cropping, and bring safe domestic supplies to the villages.

Flood Protection

Flood protection may best be exemplified by the Brahmaputra Right Bank Embankment Project

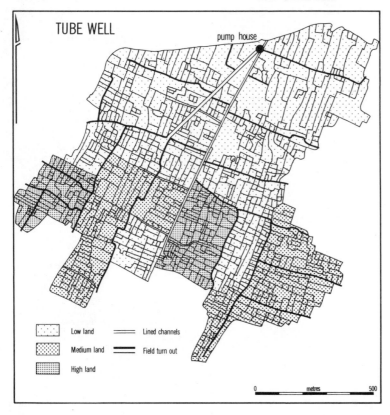

TUBE WELL

pump house

Low land   Lined channels

Medium land   Field turn out

High land

0   metres   500

FIG. 7.8 A tubewell irrigation system.
The location of the pump house on
relatively low land requires that the lined
channels and some field turn-outs to higher
land be raised a few feet above the surrounding fields.

TABLE 7.4

Crop Areas Dacca–Demra Scheme

	Pre-project ha	Pre-project acres	1969–70 ha	1969–70 acres	Pre-project yields kg/ha	Pre-project yields lb/acre	1969–70 yields kg/ha	1969–70 yields lb/acre
Bhadoi crops								
Broadcast mixed aus–aman	177	437			1,106	987		
Broadcast aus			1,584	3,913			1,845	1,645
Transplanted aus			1,338	3,305			2,582/5,072*	2,303/4,525*
Jute			132	325				
Others			121	300				
	177	437	3,175	7,843				
Aman crops								
Broadcast aman	4,492	11,091	1,330	3,286	1,383	1,234	1,752	1,563
Transplanted aman			3,068	7,580			2,675/6,363*	2,386/5,677*
	4,492	11,091	4,398	10,866				
Rabi crops								
Wheat	53	132	24	60	461	412	1,290/2,030*	1,152/1,810*
Others (?)	1,220	3,014	211	521				
Boro			3,377	8,344			2,490/5,717*	2,221/5,101*
	1,273	3,146	3,612	8,925				
Total crops	5,942	14,674	11,185	27,634				
Cropping intensity	100%		188%					

* H.Y.V.

(Fig. 7.9). Begun in 1963, the project now comprises 217 km (135 miles) of bank extending south from Kaunia on the lower Tista to the Hurasagar by which the Karatoya, Baral and Atrai systems drain to the Brahmaputra–Jamuna. The right bank area was subject to chronic flooding from the overspilling Brahmaputra–Jamuna, and from filling of the backswamp depression belt between this river and the Barind by local drainage plus occasional overflow from the Tista. Relief from the threat of deep flooding has allowed farmers to increase the acreage of higher yielding transplanted aman by 35 per cent. While in the short run the area under rice has fallen slightly, production has risen through improved yields particularly of aus and transplanted aman. Farmers in some areas protected against floods and with consequently better drainage of local rainfall, now find themselves short of moisture, a situation which can probably be righted soon by drilling tubewells. The achievement of the full potential of the project has been delayed by damage to the embankments. This situation underlies the fact that investment of large sums on capital engineering works may be vitiated unless adequate provision is made for repair and maintenance.

The necessity to integrate with flood control projects the development of irrigation if the full advantages of the capital investment in the former are to be realised is illustrated in the completed Dacca–Narayanganj–Demra Project and the Chandpur Project still under construction.

The Dacca–Demra scheme (for short) (Fig. 7.10) involves 6000 ha (14,732 acres) now surrounded by a protective embankment which keeps out floods from the Lakhya and Burhiganga Rivers. A pump station removes surplus rainwater during the monsoon, and in the dry season raises water from the Lakhya to a main canal from which 4000 ha (10,000 acres (net)) were irrigated in 1969–70. The changes in cropping brought about by the scheme are summarised in Table 7.4.

Close control of water at all seasons is responsible for the substantial switch to bhadoi and rabi cropping, and from broadcast to transplanted aman. The area is close to Dacca and so able to get the maximum attention of extension officers and a good share of the necessary inputs of seed and fertiliser. Thus it can be regarded as a demonstration plot for the nation, and can be proud of nearly doubling the area under crops, increasing cropping intensity so that 88 per cent of the land carries a second crop, and increasing the total output of food grains more than fourfold to about 274,320 t (270,000 lgt).

The *Chandpur Project* area on the east bank of the Meghna River in Comilla and Noakhali proposes to protect 30,350 ha (75,000 acres) net from flooding by the construction of 96·6 km (60 miles) of embankment. Much of the area floods to a

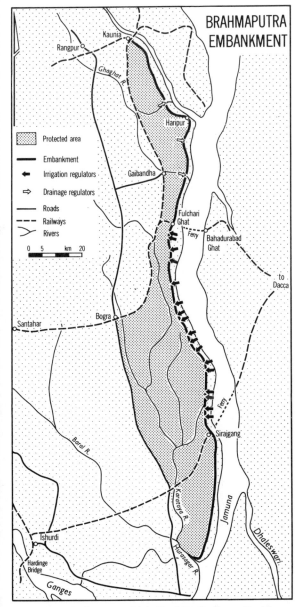

BRAHMAPUTRA EMBANKMENT

Protected area
Embankment
Irrigation regulators
Drainage regulators
Roads
Railways
Rivers

0 5 km 20

FIG. 7.9 Brahmaputra Right Bank Embankment Project.

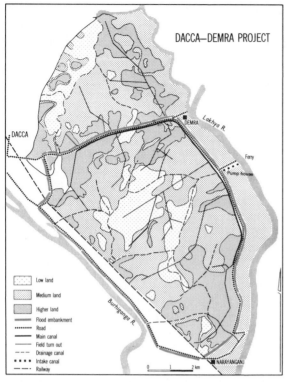

DACCA–DEMRA PROJECT

Low land
Medium land
Higher land
Flood embankment
Road
Main canal
Field turn out
Drainage canal
Intake canal
Railway

FIG. 7.10 Dacca–Demra Project. All the medium and low land within the flood embankment would previously have been inundated in normal flood periods. The pump house is located where the intake canal (from the Ferry on Lakhya River) meets the embankment.

depth of more than 1·2 m (4 ft) from early July to early November so limiting cultivation to low-yielding broadcast aman at this season, following an early aus crop. The area is among the most densely populated in Bangladesh (880 per sq km: over 2300 per sq mile). Ultimately it should be capable of carrying two crops per year of high-yielding rice, irrigated or drained of surplus water by six powerful pumps (totalling 1135 cusec) and four tidal sluices.

Salinity Control

Coastal Embankment Projects have been undertaken for several decades and now over 3000 km (1900 miles) of bank with sluice gates protect 760,000 ha (1·9 million acres) from salt water ingress throughout the Saline Tidal Delta and the main, estuarine islands of Bhola, Hatai and Sandwip. For optimal use of the land it is not sufficient merely to keep out saline water. Excess rain flood-water may have to be removed from the polder if controlled irrigation of transplanted H.Y.V. aman is to succeed, and ideally fresh water should be introduced to support a rabi or a bhadoi crop. This may be very costly to achieve in many parts of the delta. The possibility of spreading Brahmaputra–Jamuna water more evenly through the Saline Tidal Delta has been mentioned above. Figure 7.11 shows

37. Pump house at Demra: six pumps are designed to extract surplus water from the cultivated area during the rainy season and to reverse the flow to irrigation supply in the dry season. (See Fig. 7.10.)

a polder scheme in Patharghata, at the mouths of the Bishkhali and Baleswar Rivers in Patuakhali District.

THE CULTIVATORS' SOCIO-ECONOMIC ENVIRONMENT

As important to agricultural development as the physical conditions in the farmer's fields is the socio-economic system within which he operates. To the extent that this system is rooted in tradition, it proves more difficult to change than the physical and material aspect of agriculture.

Holdings are small and generally fragmented. According to a recent estimate 90 per cent of the land is in holdings of less than 25 *bighas* (c. 3·4 ha: 8·3 acres) and 99 per cent of agricultural families hold less than this figure, which is the level below which land revenue is not charged. A ceiling of 100 bighas (13·4 ha: 33 acres) has been set to a family's holding and the excess is to be acquired for distribution to landless agricultural workers and to those with under 1½ acres. Some 806,900 ha (200,000 acres) should become available for distribution.

Many cultivators rent some or all of the land they farm, either on a regular renewable basis or under an annual share cropping arrangement by which the owner gets one half of the crop (except on charland where the risks are high and only one third of the crop is taken).

For this reason the size of the area constituting an agricultural enterprise is probably impossible to estimate accurately. The agricultural census of 1960 gave the following data:

	Per cent of total	Cumulative per cent
Holdings under 0·2 ha (0·5 acres)	13	13
Holdings 0·2 to 1 ha (0·5 to 2·4 acres)	39	52
Holdings 1 to 2 ha (2·4 to 4·9 acres)	26	78
Holdings over 2 ha (over 5 acres)	22	100

Districts where holdings over 2 ha (5 acres) much exceed the national average of 22 per cent of the total are Dinajpur (49 per cent) where agricultural colonisation by clearing of *terai* jungle has been proceeding in recent decades, Kushtia (46 per cent), Rajshahi (37 per cent) and Jessore (34 per cent). All are border districts to India and the figure may reflect the effects of out-migration by Hindu landowners after partition. Relatively low proportions of these larger holdings are recorded for Chittagong (11 per cent), Comilla (6·5 per cent) and Noakhali (9 per cent), all districts of high population pressure on land resources.

At the other end of the scale, while an average 13 per cent of holdings are under 0·2 ha (0·5 acres), high proportions are found in Chittagong (28 per cent), Comilla (23 per cent), Faridpur (26 per cent) and Noakhali (24 per cent), and low proportions in Bogra (5 per cent), Chittagong Hill Tract (3 per cent), Kushtia (4 per cent) and Rangpur (5 per cent).

Another statistic indicative of the shortage of land is that there is at present less than 4·5 ha (1·1 acres) per farm *worker*, and less than 0·13 ha (one third of an acre) per head of population on the basis of cultivated land and population estimated for 1969–70. The population employed in agriculture may be classified as follows:

	Per cent
Owning all land tilled	36
Part owning, part renting	9·4
Renting all land tilled	1·3
Share-cropping	3·6
Landless agricultural labouring	17·5
Unpaid helper	32·6

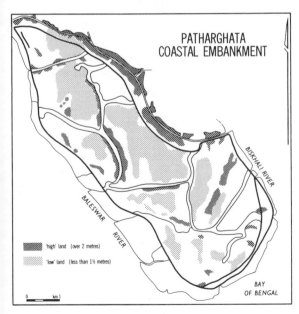

FIG. 7.11 Patharghata Coastal Embankment. This encloses a typical polder, protecting it from inflow of saline water, particularly in the dry season.

38. Agricultural labourers' home: two metres square, 1·5 m high. Made of bamboo and rice straw, it stands in a corner of the landlord's compound.

Landless labourers numbered 2·6 million, and formed as much as 32 per cent of all workers in Barisal District, and as little as 10 per cent in Comilla.

Fragmentation of holdings into a number of non-contiguous plots is the rule. In 1960 more than half of the holdings were divided into six or more fragments. Unfortunately Muslim customary law entitles every heir to a share of an estate, and it is difficult to prevent holdings becoming uneconomically small and increasingly fragmented. For efficient farming the holdings should be consolidated, but this is an immense task even if the owners can be persuaded to agree to it. Small holdings limit the owner's capacity to borrow credit for improvements.

Some of these disadvantages of the land-holding system are being overcome under various types of co-operative scheme. The low-lift and tubewell irrigation projects have encouraged farmers to co-operate to be able to obtain a share of the water. At Comilla the Rural Academy specialises in research into co-operative farming and systems to provide rural credit. Modernised farming is providing the incentive for experimentation in new forms of co-operative management. It is at the level of the farming group perhaps pooling its land, labour and other resources and sharing the product in proportion to these inputs, that a successful adaptation of scientific methods to a still very traditional socio-economic environment must be worked out. Traditionally credit is raised against the security of land or other property. If progress is to be made by the tenant or share-cropper, ways must be found for him to raise a loan, at a reasonable rate of interest, against the value of the crop yet to be sown.

CHAPTER EIGHT

POPULATION AND CITIES

POPULATION

Bangladesh shows little, if any, sign of reducing the very high rates of population increase that characterise agricultural countries of the under-developed world. At the 1961 census, Bangladesh had a population of 50·8 million, compared with 42·1 million in 1951. The 1961 figure is now considered to have been considerably understated, but even at its face value the population was increasing at 2·4 per cent annually. Provisional figures from the 1974 census give the total as 71·3 million, representing an annual rate of increase of 3·09 per cent since 1961.

Population increase is a function of death rates as well as of birth rates, and the former have fallen as health has gradually improved, to a level of 17 per thousand, compared with around 30 at the time of the partition of India in 1947. Because of this downward trend in death rates and the slower decline anticipated in birth rates (births per woman declined from 7 to 6·5 between 1960 and 1970) the annual rate of increase in population is expected to *increase* to 3·4 per cent in the 1980s before it ultimately falls to a level between a high estimate of 2·9 per cent and a low of 1·7 per cent by the end of the century, when the total might be as high as 175 million or as low as 140 million. Whether either target will be reached will depend on the country being free from war, pestilence and famine. Whether the standard of living enjoyed by the people will show any improvement a quarter of a century hence depends largely on their ability to apply energetically to their farming the technology already available today.

Bangladesh demonstrates the typically broad-based population pyramid of the under-developed country. Half the population is under 15 years of age, putting a great strain on the economically active section to provide for the children, the aged and the largely under-employed women so prevalent in a Muslim society which still maintains the custom of 'purdah', or veiling of women, which discourages their free movement and participation in wage-earning activity.

After births and deaths, migration is the third factor impinging on total population numbers and growth rates. The troubled months of 1971 following the 'army crackdown' in March led several millions of the population to migrate to seek refuge in India. The number involved is variously estimated but could have been as high as 12 million. Within a few months of independence being realised in December 1971, the bulk of the refugees were reported to have returned to Bangladesh.

Late in 1973 and continuing into 1974 there were taking place exchanges of people between Bangladesh and Pakistan, which may slightly affect the numbers and composition of the population. Some 150,000 Bangalees, stranded in Pakistan were returning to Bangladesh, while Pakistan was accepting from Bangladesh not only repatriated West Pakistanis, but 'a substantial number', probably up to about 100,000 of the so-called Biharis, non-Bangalees who did not wish to remain in the new Bangalee nation state.

POPULATION DENSITY

Bangladesh is among the most crowded corners of the world by any criterion and among the nations dependent on agriculture it is probably the most densely populated. While agriculture remains very largely a subsistence activity the population density

39.   Palanquin carrying a Muslim lady observing purdah.

distribution reflects the capacity of the land to support cultivators using traditional skills. The existence of industrial cities undoubtedly affects the pattern since these represent concentrations of job opportunities which attract population to themselves and to their immediate vicinity, and which create economic demands for food, other goods and services, stimulating the development of surrounding areas and so increasing their carrying capacity.

POPULATION DENSITY
1961

per square km less than 231	per square ml less than 600	per square km 348–420	per square ml 900–1099
231–347	600–899	421–578	1100–1499
		over 578	over 1500

0 kilometres 100

Fig. 8.1   Population density: 1961 census, by thanas.

In considering this question it is helpful to examine not only the static picture in as recent a population density map as possible but also to try to identify the changes in distribution that seem to be taking place. The crude distribution pattern in 1961 is seen in Fig. 8.1 and the pattern of change in Fig. 8.2. In Fig. 8.3 the estimated population in 1970 is related to the total area of crops grown in 1969–70.

The map of overall density of population shows by its shading in which quintile a thana occurs (one fifth of the thanas fall into each quintile). There is a remarkable concentration of areas in the upper quintile in the southeastern quarter of the country in a block taking in all of Comilla, most of Noakhali and a large part of Dacca District and extending into Mymensingh and Faridpur. The remaining thanas in the upper quintile (with over 580 persons per sq km, 1500 per square mile) may mostly be seen as clusters close to the main block as in Barisal and Pabna, or associated with industrial areas as in Chittagong and Khulna.

That one is dealing with a phenomenon of regional significance is borne out by the fact that the thanas in the second quintile of densities are for the most part contiguous with those in the upper quintile. Together the two quintiles presumably indicate the regional pattern of high agricultural productivity. Areas of transplanted aman, aus and often jute cultivation are associated with soil annually rejuvenated by floodwaters.

At the other end of the scale appear most of the problem areas. The two lower quintiles include all the Chittagong Hill Tracts and the adjoining thanas mainly south of Cox's Bazar where jungle-covered uplands reduce the effective agricultural area.

Similarly ranked are the thanas in the Saline Tidal Delta with considerable sectors of the Sundarbans Forest and those along the sea face in Patuakhali District and in the Meghna Estuary. A good deal of the northeast complex, including the Meghna Depression and the swampy zone marginal to the Shillong Plateau falls into this category of low population density. Along the western flank of the country most of Dinajpur District in the less favoured part of the North Bengal Sandy Alluvial Fan, the Barind, the Atrai–Chalan Bil depression and the Moribund Delta have less than 347 persons per sq km (900 per square mile).

Changes in population density between the last two census of 1951 and 1961 are shown in Fig. 8.2. The average increase was 21·2 per cent. Comparing this map with that of 1961 population density it is noteworthy that only one quarter of the thanas in the two upper quintiles of population increase occur also in the two upper quintiles of population density. Population increase was most marked in the west and northwest where densities were generally low especially away from the Barind. Urban areas

and thanas peripheral to the four larger cities show strong increases, but through the most densely populated regions of Comilla, Noakhali, the Meghna and Padma plains of Mymensingh and Dacca the increase was about or below average. This suggests that these areas had reached their maximum level of carrying capacity under current agricultural methods, forcing some population to move out to find land or work elsewhere.

The pattern of cropping intensity, that is the ratio of the total area of crops grown in a year compared with the net cropped area, helps the interpretation of the maps of population density and change. Strict comparability cannot be achieved. Fig. 8.4 based on the 1944–45 *Agricultural Statistics by Plot to Plot Enumeration in Bengal* and 1947–48 data for Sylhet District, giving 'normal' estimates, shows the position at the time of partition. Fig. 8.5 uses the *Pakistan Census of Agriculture*, 1960. Both sources provide subdivisional data (except for Sylhet in 1947–48) which can be mapped to show broad regional patterns satisfactorily.

At the time of partition, the average percentage

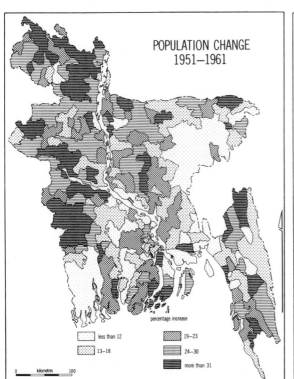

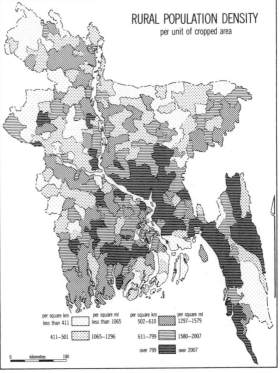

FIG. 8.2 Percentage increase in population 1951 to 1961 by thanas.

FIG. 8.3 Rural population density per unit of cropped area, 1970 estimates.

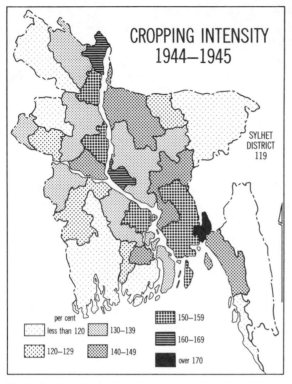

FIG. 8.4   Cropping intensity 1944–45, by subdivisions (except Sylhet District).

its already high intensity. At the other end of the scale, the regions of low intensity generally remained so, with the major exception of the non-saline tidal delta in Patuakhali.

From the available data there has been little change in overall intensity in the decade 1960–70. Some regional changes have occurred however, notably an increase in Dinajpur and Rangpur Districts in North Bengal, both in the alluvial fan and the Tista Plain, where tubewell irrigation has brought about a considerable intensification in cropping. By and large the solution to Bangladesh's problem of food supply for an increasing population lies in improving yields per hectare rather than cropping intensity.

The map of population density per total unit area of crops (Fig. 8.3) is probably the best indication of pressure of population on the land. For example, since it relates population to the total crop area in a year it takes account of double cropping. Urban areas naturally show very high densities, and it is noticeable that their influence extends to surrounding thanas, where often urban industrial workers reside in overgrown rural villages.

intensity was 131, i.e. almost one-third of the cultivated land carried more than one crop in the year. Areas with notably low cropping intensity were: the Barind with its intractable clay soils, generally impossible to plough in the dry season; the North Bengal Sandy Alluvial Fan, whose sub-surface water resources were not exploited till the last decade; the Saline Delta and South Chittagong coastal areas, where dry season cultivation is restricted by salinity; and Sylhet where severe flooding in the wet season limits cropping to the dry season in low lying areas. The highest intensities were in areas flanking the Brahmaputra–Jamuna–Padma, and in the double rice cropping region of Comilla–Noakhali.

By 1960 (Fig. 8.5) the overall cropping intensity had risen to 148. Substantial increases in intensity were in the aman–jute growing areas of the central region – in the districts of Pabna, Tangail, Kushtia, Dacca and Faridpur, flanking the Jamuna–Padma, most of which areas had above average intensities before partition. The double-rice region of Comilla –Noakhali–North Chittagong also improved on

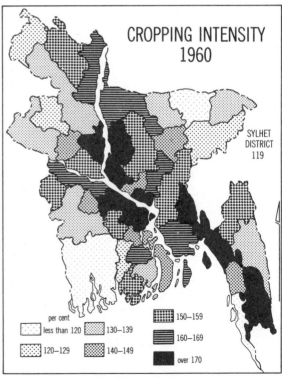

FIG. 8.5   Cropping intensity 1960, by subdivisions.

Apart from these spheres of urban industrial influence, several high density areas may be defined:

(*a*) Much of Dacca (excluding the Madhupur Tract of old alluvium), Comilla, Noakhali and Chittagong, from a near continuous region with rural *man : crop* densities generally over 811 per sq km (2100 per sq mile) and in several instances, well beyond the commuter range of industrial towns, exceeding or reaching 1158 per sq km (close to 3000 per sq mile).

(*b*) The Tidal Delta, away from the coast, whether saline or not, has most of its thanas in the upper two quintiles with over 618 per sq km (1600 per sq mile) of crops.

(*c*) Flanking the Jamuna in Pabna and Tangail Districts.

(*d*) A block of thanas in eastern Faridpur.

A common feature to all these areas is their ability to grow aman paddy, usually transplanted aman, and in the highest density areas aus features significantly as an additional food crop. Rainfall and/or floodwaters are relatively reliable and given water retentive soils conditions are good for paddy cultivation.

However, the high density areas are those least able to feed themselves (Fig. 5.1). This fact, taken with the knowledge that in the region concerned cropping intensity is generally over 150 per cent, and extensively over 170 per cent, strongly suggests that population pressure has been the incentive to striving for food self-sufficiency through intensification of agriculture.

URBANISATION

Bangladesh is one of the least urbanised countries in the world; for its size, probably no country is less urbanised. The 5·2 per cent of the population in towns and cities in 1961 is not even double the proportion in 1931:

1931	2·7 per cent	1951	4·4 per cent
1941	3·3 per cent	1961	5·2 per cent

This low percentage reflects the predominantly agricultural character of the country's economy, and its relative backwardness in terms of development. Dacca, the capital and largest city, had only 556,712 inhabitants at the 1961 census. In 1941,

before partition, it had 239,728, as a district town in the Province of Bengal the capital of which was the multi-millionaire conurbation of Calcutta. Partition in 1947 made Dacca a provincial capital; independence in 1971 brought metropolitan city status, and its population was probably over 900,000 (or 1·3 million if Narayanganj (*c.* 400,000) is regarded as part of its conurbation). Chittagong follows with about 600,000, then Khulna with 250,000 (or may be 400,000). Apart from these probably only Barisal now tops the 100,000 mark (Fig. 1.1) which is the census limit for cities.

Thus, in the early 1970s between 3 and 3·2 per cent of the population were in cities of over 100,000. At the 1961 census 4·35 per cent were in towns of 20,000 or more which would have placed Bangladesh very low in the table of world urbanisation, well behind India, Sri Lanka, Burma, Indonesia and Thailand. While the absolute percentage may have improved slightly since 1961, there is no reason to suppose that the relative position of Bangladesh in this regard has changed significantly.

At the 1961 census the town size distribution of the 78 towns was this:

Over 100,000	4
50,000	5
25,000	15
10,000	23
5,000	21
Less than 5,000	10

The estimates for the 1970s are necessarily liable to considerable error. While the capital has probably attracted numbers of refugees, the problems of rehabilitating industry after the war may have held back growth in Chittagong, Narayanganj and Khulna. In a country of mainly subsistent agriculturalists there is a tendency for the population to respond to crisis by returning in large numbers to their villages where at least a share of the family's food grain production can be expected.

The majority of towns are simply local markets with some administrative functions, maybe collecting and processing agricultural products for internal or overseas trade. However, factories processing commodities such as sugar cane, tea, or growing and baling raw jute are not always associated with urban settlements within the census definition

78 BANGLADESH

ALL AREAS

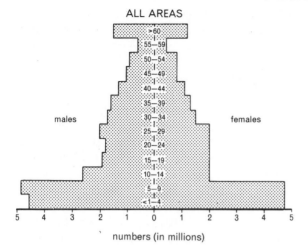

numbers (in millions)

URBAN AREAS

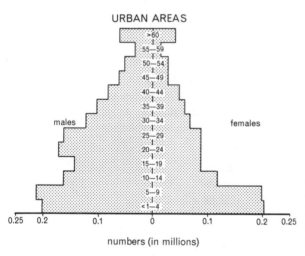

numbers (in millions)

RURAL AREAS

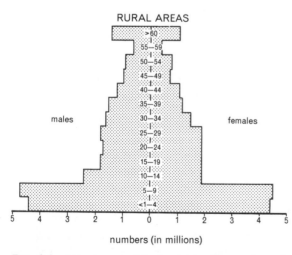

numbers (in millions)

FIG. 8.6 Age–sex pyramids for total, urban and rural population, 1961 census.

of 5000 inhabitants and may be large semi-industrial villages.

The process of urbanisation, by which the proportion of the total population living in towns increases, affects first the male working group in the community who go to the urban centres to find work in the new industries that should accompany development. In Bangladesh there is still a clear imbalance in the sex and age ratios of the urban population reflecting this process since many males migrate without their wives and families. In the five largest cities there are between 532 and 676 females per 1000 males. In the cases of Chittagong and Khulna the sex ratio had deteriorated in the intercensal period, 1951–61, suggesting the strongly industrial and impermanent character of the migration by workers. In Dacca (667), Narayanganj (592) and Barisal (676) the ratio showed some improvement.

Among the 20 towns with between 25,000 and 100,000 inhabitants the sex ratio was below 700 in only one (Barisal), and better than 800 in 13. Similarly, among 23 towns in the range 10,000 to 25,000 only one, the Kaptai Hydel Project (211), had a ratio below 745 and 18 towns had better than 800. These ratios suggest the normal pattern for the country town in which 'modern' industry is either of small importance or has been long enough established (as in the railway workshop centres) for the sex balance to have become adjusted nearer to the national level.

The small town group with under 10,000 inhabitants numbers 30 centres among which eight have ratios below 700, and six of these are exceptionally low with from 112 to 441 females per thousand males. These include Mongla Port (112), Chhatak Cement Factory (387) (recorded as urban despite its population of 577) and Chandraghona Paper Mills (376).

Figure 8.6 shows the age–sex distribution of the total, urban and rural population in 1961. The pyramid for urban population is markedly lopsided, approaching normality only in the under-10 age group, where the urban children have not yet left home. If one focuses attention on the economically most active age groups, 20–39, the urban–rural contrast is very clear whether one looks at the sex ratios as demonstrated in the age–sex pyramid or at the proportion of the total population in the age group. Over Bangladesh as a whole, 27 per cent of the population is in the age group 20–39. In the major cities this age group constitutes a much higher proportion: 38 per cent in the strongly industrial centres of Khulna and Narayanganj, 37 per cent in Chittagong and 35 per cent in Dacca. These figures reinforce the impression based upon sex ratios, that urbanisation is still largely a matter of migration by the males in the economically active age groups. Within the 20–39 age group in all urban areas males account for 65 per cent, female for 35 per cent of the total, while in the rural areas the sexes are about evenly balanced at 50·1 per cent males, 49·19 per cent females.

The map in Fig. 8.7 shows by districts the difference between the percentages of the district total population of males and females in the age groups 20–39. Four of the five districts where females

outnumber males form a block astride the Meghna estuary: Faridpur, Bakarganj (including Patuakhali), Comilla and Noakhali. These are all districts of well above average population density (Fig. 8.1) and without significant development of occupations outside agriculture. Bogra is the fifth such district, and to it may be linked Pabna with the lowest excess of male to females in these age groups (0·1 per cent difference) and the districts of Rajshahi (0·5), Mymensingh (0·3) and Sylhet (0·4) forming a belt across the north centre of the country. It is probably fair to say that all these areas represent two regions from which active males tend to move in search of employment while the other districts, with males 20–39 exceeding females 20–39 in the total population by 0·8 per cent or more, are the areas of opportunity. Certainly the districts so identified include Dacca (with the capital and industrial Narayanganj), Chittagong and Khulna (with their industrial ports), and the Chittagong Hill Tracts with the Chandraghona Paper Mills and Kaptai Hydel Project. Kushtia and Jessore are border districts which suffered some out-migration to India following partition, and may be enjoying a measure of rehabilitation helped by the Ganges–Kobadak irrigation scheme and several industrial enterprises, such as sugar mills. Dinajpur and to a lesser extent Rangpur in the far northwest had some cultivable areas available for clearing and colonisation, and in the past decade groundwater resources have begun to be exploited with considerable encouragement to intensification of agriculture.

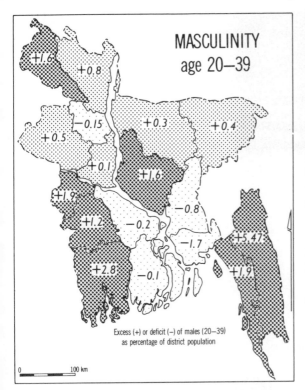

FIG. 8.7 Masculinity of the population in the age-group 20–39. The map shows the excess (+) or deficit (−) of males in the age-group 20–39 expressed as a percentage of the total population of each district. Thus in Dinajpur +1·6 is the excess of 15·6 (being the percentage of the district's population represented by males in the age-group 20–39) over 14·0 (being the percentage represented by females in the same age group).

Dacca

Dacca has long been unrivalled as the regional capital of what is now Bangladesh. Geographical centrality, reinforced by the fortunate combination of physiographic features favourable to both land and water communications with a populous and highly productive region, has ensured its status. The basic physiographic element in the site is the prong of relatively high ground that extends southwards from the Madhupur Tract to the Burhiganga River, and is flanked by low floodlands of the Turag River to the west and the Balu River to the east. The prong of flood-free terrace averages c. 6 km (about 4 miles) in width and has strongly influenced the direction of Dacca's growth, which has been generally

40.   Downtown Dacca–Motijheel
Commercial area's modern buildings.

41.   Moghul period brick building,
Lalbagh, Dacca.

northwards from the old nucleus of the pre-Moghul river port on the Burhiganga levee. It may be premature to speak of a Dacca–Narayanganj conurbation, for the two urban areas are still but tenuously linked by a strip of discontinuous built-up area along the road and railway that clings to the Burhiganga north bank. As yet Narayanganj and this strip of godowns seem to look to their rivers rather than to their land-wise connections. However such discussion is largely pointless, for whatever the physical appearances, Narayanganj is close enough to Dacca in distance and in time – (c. 12 km (less than 8 miles) separates their railway stations) – to be regarded as part of an urban continuum. Its jute mills and presses may trace their antecedents to times when the economic viewpoint of Narayanganj was more clearly separate from that of Dacca, when the former stood for the raw jute collecting and exporting trade, while the latter embodied British imperial administration of the region. However, today the Lakhya River banks at Narayanganj provide sites for power stations, boat yards and jute and cotton textile mills serving the country's internal demands in general and Dacca's in particular.

Earliest Dacca may date from the seventh century A.D. From the 13th century it was a centre of Muslim rule, and was chosen as the Moghuls' capital in the early 17th century when its preeminence in trade attracted Portuguese and other European merchants. The 18th and 19th centuries saw Dacca decline in importance as Calcutta forged ahead as the British capital of Imperial India. The early 20th century brought a brief renaissance of Dacca's significance as an administrative centre, when from 1905 to 1912 it was capital of the short-lived province of Eastern Bengal and Assam. By this time a railway link with Chittagong had been established.

Figure 8.8 shows in a simplified way the major elements in Dacca's urban growth. Moghul Dacca stretched along the Burhiganga for about 6 km (4 miles) with several forts sited close to the river – then the town's *raison d'être*. This belt is now the most congested area of Dacca and contains the older section of the central business district alongside the river port at Sadarghat. Characteristically when the railway arrived from the north along the old alluvial prong it swung east to skirt the older built up area *en route* to Narayanganj. Recently the

railway has been realigned east of the city to avoid several level crossings within the growing city which had become the location of chronic frustrating delays. Development of Dacca as a British provincial capital led to the layout of stately administrative buildings and comfortable European bungalows in large gardens in the Ramna area in the bend of the old railway line. This suburb remains one of high class residences, though more modern development has extended to the west (Dhanmandi) and north (Gulshan Model Town). Government administration has outgrown its quarters in Ramna and is to be largely relocated in the 'Second Capital' area in the northwest.

Industry in Dacca before 1947 was closely tied to the banks of the Burhiganga (and to Narayanganj). Independence brought new vigour to the city, now capital of a province of Pakistan, freed from subservience to India's Calcutta. While expansion in the jute industry took place still along the Burhiganga and the Lakhya rivers – for water transport is still essential to that trade – new manufacturing plants were set up in an industrial estate alongside the railway and roads in Tejgaon.

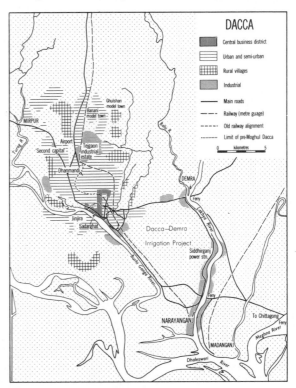

FIG. 8.8 Dacca.

42.   Street market: buttons, pens, spoons. Each vendor occupies about a metre of pavement.

43.   Dacca Sadarghat waterfront: 'bustee' shelters along foreshore occupied by homeless families; country boats and ferry steamer.

It is of interest to note how the main business area has migrated from the vicinity of Sadarghat to the administrative district east of Ramna. Dacca's C.B.D., or for that matter any of its retail trading centres, should not be thought of as replicas of shopping areas in western cities. There are virtually no large stores, but rather a vast number of rival shops, book shops and so on. It is only in the close together, and similarly cloth shops, variety shops, book shops, and so on. It is only in the offices of banks and other business corporations and government departments that the C.B.D. resembles more closely its western counterparts.

Reference has been made to the well-defined high class residential areas on non-flooding land. Towards the other end of the social scale, low class housing is crowded into the old city area along the Burhiganga, and is left with the low-lying lands on the east and west flanks of the terrace prong. The absolute nadir of squalor is suffered by the squatters, many of them refugees, who crowd into 'bustee' encampments of make-shift shelters wherever vacant land can be occupied without immediate eviction. The track of the now abandoned railway and vacant building blocks adjacent to the modern C.B.D. are typical examples of squatter settlements, but the scourge is widespread throughout the more open parts of the city. Cycle rickshaw drivers and their mechanics, and street-stall vendors of *pan* and cigarettes sleep in rough shelters on the roadside.

A type of residential area rare in modern western cities (but represented in the workers' tenements of mid-19th-century Britain, for example) is found in association with the large jute mills which build cramped colonies for their employees, which often take on the character of men's dormitories.

An indication of the conditions in which the poorer classes live in Dacca, and for that matter in most South Asian cities, may be had from the fact that in Lalbagh, part of the Old City, only 5 per cent of the houses had electricity and 13 per cent had water in 1961. In the squatter settlements there are practically no services whatsoever; the residents have to draw water from stand-pipes in the road and many have access to no latrine. To judge from the experience of expanding metropolitan cities in Asia the problem of squatter settlement is likely to increase rather than otherwise in the probably long years of transition to development, while the surplus of people on the land continues to grow at a rate far faster than that of the growth in alternative jobs. Meanwhile Dacca will expand in area and population, and the most probable direction of urban extension is northwards to form a linear city to link with industrial settlement at Tungi where the metre gauge railway forks to Mymensingh and Chittagong. Narayanganj is likely also to expand along both banks of the Lakhya, a development encouraged by the new branch railway from Narsingdi which enables traffic to by-pass Dacca's congested yards. The persistence of river communications nonetheless seems assured.

44. Workers' housing at a large jute mill near Dacca.

Chittagong

Chittagong is more clearly than Dacca the product of past economic imperialism, and its predominant characteristic today is probably its commercialism. As the only port in the country with wharves and the potentiality for rapid development at the time of partition, Chittagong has expanded very rapidly from a population of 91,301 in 1941 to perhaps 600,000. The core of the city lies where the ridges of the Sitakund Hills approach close to the Karnaphuli River and provide a dry site (Fig. 8.9). Here the Portuguese established a settlement in the early 16th century, probably more for the convenience of a river anchorage and revictualling point within the general trading realm of the Bay of Bengal than for any specific commodity available locally. The core area with its tributary creek, Chaktai Khal, providing access right into the

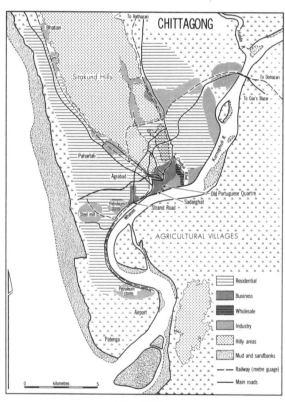

FIG. 8.9 Chittagong.

town for large country boats which can lie on their keels at low tide, may be compared with the Sadarghat area of Dacca, where the traditional business district lies. The railway came to the edge of the core but its branch along Strand Road following the right bank of the river better explains its construction which was to serve the tea industry of Assam. Before partition four jetties on Strand Road handled mainly tea and some jute. Before the Kaptai Hydel Project was completed, the discharge of the Karnaphuli at Chittagong fell to as little as 204,000 m³/h (2000 cusecs) in the dry season, and the maximum anticipated safe draft for shipping was sometimes less than 6 m (20 ft) in February. Control of the river flow for power development was expected to raise the minimum flow to 1,630,000 m³/h (16,000 cusecs) and the minimum draft by about 0·6 m (2 ft) above the previous level. Now there are 17 wharves. A modern C.B.D. is evolving closer to the dock area, and beyond it some industries are spreading out across Patenga Peninsula, e.g. the steel rolling mill, oil refineries and oil storage tank farms.

Chittagong has grown up only on the right bank of the river which is on the outside of a meander, giving deeper water close to the bank. Because of the Sitakund Hills, industrial development has tended to align itself along the railway (and road) from Dacca–Comilla along the coastal plain, and near the branch lines to Dohazari and Hathazari. For several miles along the Dacca line factories, mainly jute textile mills, are strung out at the base of the Sitakund Hills.

A feature of Chittagong's settlement pattern is the considerable amount of impermanent bamboo frame housing, mostly on low ground, These urban villages may best be regarded as the invasion of the urban area by traditional rural styles of construction. They represent the transition in ways of life from village to town, and are gradually giving place to more permanent concrete structures. High class residences seek high point sites in the dissected hills, to catch the refreshing breezes of summer, and views out over the Bay of Bengal or inland to the Hill Tracts.

CHAPTER NINE

INDUSTRY AND COMMUNICATIONS

INDUSTRIALISATION

Bangladesh has a superabundance of unskilled labour. In most other necessities for modern industry the country is grossly deficient. Its major raw material, jute, is a product of agriculture, and much of its industry is directed to processing the output of its farms, forests and fisheries. There is a considerable small-scale craft industry in cotton textiles, metal work, leather and wood, representing the survival of traditional cottage industries. Almost all large-scale manufacturing industry has been established since partition in 1947, most of it in jute and cotton textiles.

Until the early 1950s it looked as if the country's sole indigenous source of power would be in the hydroelectric potential of the rivers of the Chittagong Hill Tracts. With the construction of the Kaptai Hydel Project on the Karnaphuli 80,000 kW capacity was harnessed, later to be increased to 120,000 kW. All other power generated was then on the basis of imported fuels. However, the picture changed dramatically, certainly as far as potential is concerned, with the discovery of natural gas in several localities. Known reserves could maintain a consumption of 22·7 million m³ (800 million cubic feet) per day for 20 years. With current use at less than 1·4 million m³ (50 million cubic feet) daily some export trade can be contemplated. The gas fields are mainly in Sylhet District and the adjacent corner of Comilla, the latter conveniently located for linkage by pipe line to Dacca. The principal industries based directly on natural gas are the nitrogenous fertiliser factories at Fenchuganj (Sylhet) and Ghorasal (Dacca) which produced 374,000 t (380,000 lgt) of urea in 1973–74. The Chhatak cement works using limestone from just over the border in India is now powered by local natural gas.

Mention may be made of two potential resources for fuel, neither likely to attract urgent exploitation while natural gas is so abundantly available. Coal has been proved in quantity and at workable depth (within c. 600 m (2000 ft)) in Bogra District. Peat deposits in swamps in Faridpur and Khulna and extensively in the Meghna Depression are a vast reserve of low grade fuel. Operating difficulties at low-lying sites in a monsoon climate which inundates every hollow in the land are a formidable and at present probably an economically unsurmountable problem.

Natural gas now accounts for almost 40 per cent of the power consumed, hydroelectricity for 36 per cent and imported oil for the remainder. The main centres for power generation and consumption are Kaptai (supplying Chittagong), Dacca–Narayanganj, Khulna and Fenchuganj. The Bheramara thermal station powers the Ganges–Kobadak pump house, while small independent units feed the small towns throughout the country. A power grid between Kaptai, Chittagong and Dacca's major thermal station at Siddirganj has been established but has proved vulnerable to cyclone damage. By 1970 installed capacity was about 670,000 kW, one fifth of it being at the Kaptai H.E.P. station. For the vast majority of the population electricity is an unimagined luxury enjoyed by the wealthy few who live in cities.

The inventory of modern industry is all too short. Before 1947 the country was an economic tributary of Calcutta, and had a few cotton textile mills, a cement works and factories processing its raw agricultural produce for export: tea factories and jute presses. Within unseparated Pakistan industrialisation developed slowly at first. Jute mills at Dacca–Narayanganj, Khulna and Chittagong had 22,000 looms in 35 factories producing 636,000 t (626,000 lgt) of goods in 1969–70, mostly sacking and with 80 per cent for export. This product finds a diminishing demand on world markets as bulk handling of grains and similar formerly bagged commodities becomes more widespread. Bangladesh has a smaller share than its rival India of the more lucrative trade in broadloom carpet backing. Plastics such as polypropelene have invaded the market, and there are serious doubts whether jute can regain and retain its traditional fields. However, one beneficial outcome of the high oil prices resulting from the current world petroleum crisis could be that users of petrochemically based synthetic fibres may be persuaded to return to natural jute products. The output of manufactured jute goods is expected to reach 535,400 t (527,000 lgt) in 1973–74 and to achieve pre-independence levels by 1975. Cotton textile mills with 750,000 spindles and 7000 looms depend on imported raw cotton or yarn, and weave to serve the huge home market. Cotton yarn production, 42 million kg (93 million lb) in 1973–74 was a little short of the pre-independence level, but cloth output at 68·6 million m (75 million yd), was already ahead. In 1969–70, the Bangalee industry was barely a quarter the size of that in West Pakistan, which with a comparable local mar-

45.   Sylhet No. 2 gas exploration well.

ket had considerable surpluses for export. The large cotton mills mainly in and near Dacca and Chittagong, but also scattered in a dozen towns throughout the country, tended like the jute industry to be the preserve of West Pakistani capital. There seems little doubt that for one reason or another it was difficult for Bangalees to gain a footing as entrepreneurs in manufacturing industry. It has been argued that East Pakistan was managed as a protected market for goods made in the West wing, which made it hard for Bangalees to gain industrial experience, and furthermore denied to the country wage-earning opportunities vital to economic development. These were among the roots of the feelings of national exploitation by West Pakistanis that underlay the urge for Bangalee independence.

The Pakistan Third Five Year Plan, 1965–69, made belated efforts to give the east wing a fairer share in investment capital. A steel rolling mill of 254,000 t (250,000 lgt) capacity (based on all imported material) and an oil refinery to process 1·52 million t (1·5 million lgt) per year were set up at Chittagong. In 1973–74 steel output was 88,000 t. A paper mill at Chandraghona on the Karnaphuli River using bamboo cut in the Chittagong Hills, hoisted past the Kaptai H.E.P. dam and rafted

46. Jute press, Narayanganj, for reducing the volume of jute bales for export.

47. Loose skeins of jute fibre being unloaded from a country boat at a jute mill at Narayanganj. In the background is a large 'flat' or cargo barge.

48.   Jute mill – weaving gunny for sacking.

49.   Workers' housing at Chandraghona Paper Mills. Note the dried cowdung cakes on the roof to left for fuel, and the efforts to grow papaya, etc.

downstream, has been in production since the 1950s with a capacity of 30,480 t (30,000 lgt). At Khulna, softwood from the Sundarbans forest is used to make newsprint and hardboard, and at Ishurdi (Pabna) high quality paper is made from bagasse, the fibrous residue of sugar cane processing. A further paper mill was being established at Chhatak near Sylhet to use bamboo, swamp reeds and jute waste.

Other industries include 15 sugar mills (mostly in the north and west: see Fig. 5.12b) handling 1016–1524 t (1000–1500 lgt) of cane per day as a rule and supplying the internal market, and the 95 tea factories located mostly in Sylhet District. Refined sugar production at 91,440 t (90,000 lgt) provides 10,160 t (10,000 lgt) for export. Leather tanning is important around Dacca and Chittagong and there is a considerable export trade

50. Jute mill near Narayanganj, showing the bungalows of supervisory staff in the foreground.

51. Stacks of raw jute at a Chittagong mill.

52. Bidi making at Bheramara, Kushtia District. Bidis are small cheap cigarettes made by packing dry tobacco 'chaff' into a rolled piece of tobacco leaf. Twenty bidis might cost a few pence/cents. The industry is notorious for its low wage rates.

in hide and skins. Narayanganj has a shoe factory but this industry is still largely a domestic craft. Wood working is widespread as a craft industry, and at Chittagong, Narayanganj, Barisal and Khulna boat building is carried on to serve the river transportation and fishing industries. Plywood factories at Chandraghona produce tea chests.

It will be noted that much of Bangladesh's industry is tied to processing local materials in a fairly simple fashion. Sophisticated industries such as mechanical engineering, in particular, are little developed as yet, but have enormous potential to satisfy the market for agricultural pumps and other machinery and the internal transport industries that must expand in the near future. Engineering is mainly confined to railway and marine repair workshops. Lack of trained manpower has long been a handicap to progress, but an engineering university at Dacca and a general realisation of the importance of technical education to development promise better for the future.

Government policy towards industrial development is based on the socialist philosophy of the new nation. Large-scale enterprise is to be state-owned and managed, while the private investor may engage in enterprise with assets not exceeding Tk. 30 million. Foreign private investment will be permitted only in enterprises in which government holds at least 51 per cent equity. For small and cottage industries private enterprise will be encouraged and their ` production integrated with large-scale industry.

COMMUNICATIONS

As a country develops economically, production of commodities, goods and services for sale becomes more important to the individual entrepreneur than mere self-sufficiency. Specialisation in production increases, and the interchange of goods between regions becomes essential. Thus development requires facilities for transportation, of commodities as well as of people.

Bangladesh suffers more than most countries from geographical handicaps to communications. Not only is its territory quartered by great rivers

(Fig. 9.1), exceedingly expensive to bridge, but for several months of the year these rivers and the deluge of monsoon rainfall on the near-level surface of the delta plains cause floods which further aggravate the problem. The extremes of seasonality add greatly to the costs of transportation. Much motor transport is rendered immobile by floods and heavy rain in the wet season, when boats can ply in almost any direction across country. Alternately in the dry season river boats are limited to the deeper channels, and the roads come into their own again.

For most Bangalee farmers a small boat takes the place of the farm cart of western peasant societies, and a large part of the traffic in farm products – rice, jute, pulses, etc. – moves to market and processing plant by country boat. These are sail driven, sometimes rowed and even hauled by manpower against adverse winds. From the larger agricultural collecting centres some cargoes may move by motorised launches or paddle steamers.

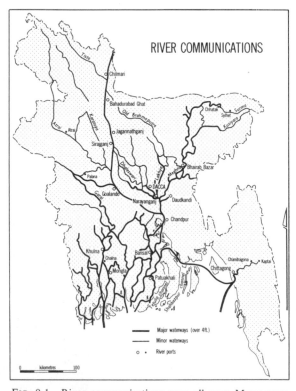

FIG. 9.1   River communications open all year. Many more channels are navigable all year round by small country boats and during the high water period from June to December by larger vessels. See Fig. 2.1 for the main rivers, all navigable by country craft.

53.   Raft of bamboo poles with a deck cargo of sunn grass for thatching: Karnaphuli River near Chittagong.

Much of the 'pucca' baled jute from the baling centres such as Narayanganj is loaded into dumb-barges or flats which are moved by motor tugs along the network of inland waterways to be loaded overside into ocean-going vessels at Chalna/ Mongla. Imported foodgrains from Chittagong port are shipped in part to Dacca by shallow draft steamers robust enough to weather the short but very occasionally stormy sea passage from the Karnaphuli mouth into the shelter of the Meghna estuary.

The map (Fig. 9.1) shows the main waterways with their minimum dry season draft. Obviously the wet season route-mileage is substantially greater than that of the dry season. Mechanised cargo boats ply on 3058 km (1900 miles) of wet season river, 2575 km (1600 miles) in the dry season, while about 8000 km (5000 miles) and 5150 km (3200 miles) represent the corresponding route distances used by country craft. Many vessels were destroyed or rendered unserviceably by the war disturbances of 1971, but the approximate cargo fleet is of the order of 2300 mechanised boats and 300,000 country craft.

Inland water transport is most important in the centre and east. Through river ports along the Jamuna, Padma and Meghna systems much cargo finds its way to metropolitan Dacca and industrial Narayanganj. The upper Meghna – the Surma and Kusiyara systems – carry cement, rocks and tea, and may again be carrying Indian cargoes under bond between Assam and Calcutta. Fast passenger-cargo steamers like the 'Rocket' service ply between Dacca–Chandpur–Barisal and Khulna, through areas practically devoid of alternative means of transportation. The northwest, the Moribund Delta and the Tippera–Chittagong plains have less need of river communications, since road and rail are relatively well developed. The Karnaphuli is however a valuable routeway inland from Chittagong, and carries bamboo and timber for the Chandraghona Paper Mills.

Railways were established during the time of British rule before the partition of India disrupted the Province of Bengal. Bangladesh has inherited parts of two railway systems, lacking compatibility of gauge, and divided in two by unbridged rivers

(Fig. 9.2). West of the Brahmaputra–Jamuna the main line network is the broad gauge relic of the line Calcutta to Jalpaiguri (terminus of the Darjeeling Hill Railway). Now it runs the length of the country, crossing the Ganges by Hardinge Bridge, and extending south to Khulna, and ultimately it is expected to Mongla Port, 19 km (12 miles) south of Chalna. Mongla is the river-anchorage on the Pusur River. Branches of broad gauge line extend to Sirajganj on the Jamuna, and south of the Ganges, through Kushtia to the river transfer point at Goalundo, and to Faridpur. In the northwest a few metre-gauge lines serve as feeders to the broad-gauge system, and through wagon ferries across the Jamuna, forge a fragile link with the railway system east of the river.

The latter system is what remained to East Pakistan of the line joining Chittagong port with the Assam tea gardens and oil field. Now it carries much of the import traffic for Dacca and the country as a whole and part of the export trade in raw and manufactured jute.

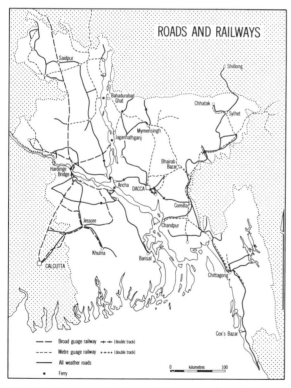

FIG. 9.2   Roads and railways. Only all-weather roads are shown. There is also a considerable length of unpaved roads passable only during the dry season.

It can be seen (Fig. 9.2) that large areas of Bangladesh lie far from railways; and, because of modern bridge building costs, are likely to remain so. Railway bridges have to be stable structures, with stable approaches. Because sandy deltaic rivers, especially the Jamuna and Padma, tend to have unstable banks and changeable courses, bridging is technically difficult and costly.

Road transport, apart from the bullock carts of the drier parts of the west, is of relatively recent importance. It was typical of the British period in many a colonial territory that the railways of the Victorian–Edwardian era remained the major means of modern communication up till the Second World War. Because of economic backwardness the motor vehicle was slow to make an impression. Add to these factors the difficulties of a terrain interlaced by waterways of seasonally variable depth and breadth – expensive to bridge for the trickle of vehicular traffic and so traversed by ferries subject to frustrating delays – and the explanation for the meagre road system becomes clearer (Fig. 9.2).

Bangladesh is thus endowed with a variety of means of surface transportation, all of them so constrained by factors of physical and economic geography that to travel between any large centres 100 km (60 miles) or more apart will almost invariably involve a journey of twice the direct distance! Only air travel can escape some of the physical obstacles, but in as poor a country it is a mode limited to the few relatively rich people and the administrators. Before the struggle for independence lost the internal airline's equipment to Pakistan, the country was developing 'air bus' services linking Dacca to Chittagong, Comilla, Sylhet, Ishurdi and Jessore. These have been largely restored.

In order to achieve a modern system of communications reaching out to every village it will be necessary to continue to develop river and road transport in particular. Hardly a thana is without access to a waterway however shallow, and this ready-made mode of communication can surely be modernised with shallow draft mechanised boats. Roads will be extended to many areas, but will inevitably suffer some interruptions due to ferries and floods. Integration of these potentially complementary systems may provide the key to Bangladesh's transport problems. The demand for

54. King George VI Bridge at Bhairab
Bazar: part-destroyed during the struggle
for independence and now repaired.
(Photo by Robson.)

55. Overcrowded transport is the rule:
country bus coming into Dacca.

transport is increasing steadily as the economy slowly emerges from stagnation; bulky food surpluses have to be moved from the northwest, imports from Chalna and Chittagong, locally manufactured fertilisers from Fenchuganj and Ghorasal, jute, raw and manufactured, from farm to factory and to the ports.

EXTERNAL COMMUNICATIONS

With restoration of friendly relationships with India it is probable that at least some of the pre-partition lines of communication will be brought back into use. The road and rail links with Calcutta, barely 64 km (40 miles) from the border, could serve to link a potential market with potential supplies in the western districts, for these areas formerly sent much fresh foodstuffs to that vast conurbation. By water the through traffic of tea and other merchandise between the Assam valley and Calcutta may revive if the river navigation services are re-established.

As a country (albeit a province) independent of India in the immediate port-partition period, East

56.   Loading jute over-side from dumb-barge at Chalna anchorage, Mongla Port on River Pusur.

Pakistan had to develop its own external trading ports. Chittagong, once a Portuguese trading post, grew from a four-jetty port in British times to a capacity of some 17 vessels alongside, and an annual throughput of over 4 million t. Chalna, although lacking wharves, grew rapidly through the 1960s to steal trade from Chittagong and to handle up to 2·6 million t of cargo annually. Chittagong dealt with most of the import traffic, and exported some jute and tea. Its oil refinery and steel plant assure its industrial development. Chalna is the more important exporter of jute, and when its rail connection with Khulna is established and wharves are built, it may well rival Chittagong more vigorously on account of its better communications with an extensive hinterland which is relatively remote from its rival.

57.   Chittagong wharves along right bank of Karnaphuli River.

CHAPTER TEN

DEVELOPMENT PROSPECTS

Bangladesh's basic problem is that common to many developing countries: how to feed an ever-increasing population while simultaneously striving to raise living standards. The prospects of achieving these ends are closely tied to the country's ability to accumulate capital funds from savings within Bangladesh or to attract capital grants or loans from abroad, or to earn foreign exchange by exporting goods and services. The extremely low level of income of the peasant farmers who make up the bulk of the economically productive population means there is little prospect of their accumulating savings, even the modest amounts needed for agricultural development. Bangladesh has very few wealthy capitalists, and much of the private capital in industry comes from West Pakistan, a source now out of the question. Foreign aid and export earnings must be the principal sources of investment capital for some years to come, a fact which accentuates the significance of jute in the Bangladesh economy. Foreign aid flowed freely to the country in the year following independence, when the disruptive effects of strife threatened economic famine and widespread suffering. Around $1000 million is estimated to have been committed in 1972, from both western and communist bloc countries, and many experts from national and international organisations were recruited to help re-establish the country's economic infrastructure.

Perhaps the most important new fact in the economic situation of Bangladesh is that severance of ties with Pakistan (some would say its stranglehold on the economy) has made possible a new relationship with India. West Pakistan was too remote for there to develop satisfactory inter-wing trade, which ran consistently to the advantage of the West wing. In 1969–70 exports from West to East Pakistan totalled Rs. 1660 million with only Rs. 920 million going in the opposite direction. The composition of that trade gives some indication of Bangladesh's capacity to export. Tea made up 26 per cent of the total, followed by jute goods, 17 per cent, and paper and paper board, 12 per cent. It may be assumed that goods in roughly these proportions may now be available for export in addition to those formerly exported to destinations other than Pakistan. Simultaneously the composition of imports from West Pakistan suggests needs which may be filled by new industry within Bangladesh, or may have to be bought from abroad. Cotton fabrics, 15 per cent, yarn and thread, 5 per cent, head the list of manufactured goods and give a measure of the economic colonialism in which Bangalees felt they lived, for cotton manufactures are well within the country's capacity to make for themselves. Food grains, 22 per cent, raw cotton, 10 per cent, oilseeds, 7 per cent, and tobacco form major items, all primary commodities. Other manufactures exported to the East were machinery, 7 per cent, pharmaceuticals, 3 per cent, tobacco, 2 per cent, and cement, 3 per cent.

Following three years of abnormality, the pattern of foreign trade of Bangladesh is taking its expected shape. In 1972–73 exports were worth Tk. 2,710 million, made up as follows:

Raw jute	37%
Jute goods	52%
Hides, skins and leather	5%
Tea	3%
Fish	1%

Other items include paper, paper board, cotton, textiles and chillies.

Imports totalled Tk. 2,264 million, comprising

as is usual in developing countries, a number of manufactured items, raw materials such as petroleum and food to support an increasing population. The 1972–73 list was as follws:

Manufactured goods	29%
Machinery and transport equipment	
Chemicals	15%
Crude materials	7%
Petroleum and petroleum products	6%
Food	15%

The future for raw and manufactured jute on world markets is as problematical as that of natural rubber. Much will depend on the ability of producers to deliver high quality jute at low cost. In this varietal research for high-yielding strains and agronomic research to establish the best ways of cultivating efficiently are necessary. If costs cannot be kept low, and if supplies of given quality cannot be guaranteed, the sophisticated industries now using the best jute will turn to synthetic alternatives. In 1966–68 Bangladesh produced a third of the world's natural jute and allied fibres, and accounted for almost half of the world export trade in raw and manufactured jute. India was close behind with 32 per cent production and 34 per cent of trade. About half of Bangladesh's jute production is exported raw after being sorted, baled and pressed at Narayanganj or Khulna. The remainder goes to local industry which exports 80 per cent of the manufactured goods. The upset of commerce during the war, followed by uncertainties and the nationalisation of trade, have hit the jute exports severely. In 1972–73, of 6·5 million bales of jute produced only 3·5 million were exported, leaving an embarrassingly large carry-over of stocks. There is a considerable but unmeasured illegal trade in smuggled jute across the border with West Bengal.

With the breach with Pakistan, Bangladesh must find new outlets for the tea surplus to domestic requirements – about half the total crop of 70 million pounds. An assured protected market in West Pakistan combined with uncertainty brought neglect of reinvestment and led to relatively high cost production which will make marketing overseas difficult. In mid-1973 it was estimated that the selling price of Bangladesh tea on the world market was Tk. 1·62 per pound, against a cost price of Tk. 3, and the industry was seen to be in serious economic difficulties. Tea exports are now subsidised by Tk. 0·75 per pound, and a good market has been opened up in the Middle East.

Judging from the value of cotton manufactured goods imported formerly, there is considerable scope for an import substitution programme. Short stapled cotton is grown in the Chittagong Hill Tracts by shifting cultivators, and sometimes there has been a surplus for export. Whether better quality cotton could be grown economically on the plains, in competition with rice and jute, is a moot point, but it is noteworthy that Dacca once had the enviable reputation of manufacturing the finest muslin fabrics from locally grown cotton.

Mention was made above of the surplus of natural gas available for export. The new rapprochement with India, whose immense industrial conurbation in Calcutta and its Hooglyside satellites lies less than 64 km (40 miles) from the nearest Bangladesh railway frontier township, presents an obvious opportunity for trade in power resources. Bangladesh needs many engineering and structural metal products manufactured in Calcutta and the Damodar Valley. In the short run it would seem clear that trade could develop to the mutual benefit of the two countries. As well as natural gas, India could readily use fish and vegetables from the adjacent districts of Bangladesh. One major difficulty may handicap trading relationships; the rival interest of both nations, in fact of both Bengals, West and Bangladesh, in jute production and manufacture.

The problems facing the young Bangladesh state are formidable indeed, and will demand of the newly independent Bangalees training in skills of technology and management, discipline, initiative and courage for which there is no substitute to be borrowed or purchased from abroad, but which must be found within the nation itself.

BIBLIOGRAPHICAL NOTE

Readers wishing to read further on Bangladesh and its antecedents are referred to the following:

General works (in date order):
El Hamza, *Pakistan, a Nation* (Lahore, 1944).
Rashid, Haroun er, *East Pakistan, a Systematic Regional Geography and its Development Planning Aspects* (Sh. Ghulam Ali & Sons, Lahore, 1965).
Tayyeb, A., *Pakistan, a Political Geography* (O.U.P., Toronto, 1966).
Spate, O. H. K. and Learmonth, A. T. A., *India and Pakistan* (Methuen, London, 1967).
Ahmed, Nafis, *An Economic Geography of East Pakistan* (O.U.P., London, 1968).
Ray, Jayarta Kumar, *Democracy and Nationalism on Trial: a study of East Pakistan* (Indian Instit. of Advanced Study, Simla, 1968).
Johnson, B. L. C., *South Asia* (Heinemann Educational Books, London, 1969).

Articles on Bangladesh appear most frequently in *The Oriental Geographer*, published continuously from 1957 by the Bangladesh (formerly East Pakistan) Geographical Society at the Department of Geography, University of Dacca.

A series of six topical maps at the scale 1 : 500,000 have been produced by the International Bank for Reconstruction and Development (1972). They cover: I. Political Divisions, II. Population, III. Hydrology, IV. Transportation, V. Land Use Associations, VI. Land Development Units.

GENERAL INDEX

For place names, rivers and regions see separate index

Entries thus: 22 refer to text; *22* refer to figures or tables; **22** refer to photographs. All are page numbers.

Age Ratios (Urban), 78–9
Aghani season, (*see* Aman season)
Agriculture, activities, 32–7, *33*; future development, 8, 12, 31, 96; innovations, 29, 32, 42, 56–72, *61*; plantation, 54–5; sedentary, 32–46; shifting (*see* Jhum cultivation); traditional, 8, 26, 29–47, **32**, **34**, **72**
Aid, foreign, 95
Air Travel, 92
Akbar (Emperor), 1
Alluvial, cones, 12; fan, 9, 10, 12, 66, 76; plains, 8, 9, 10, 11; ridge, 10, 11, 13, terraces, 9, 10, 12, 35
Aman, *57*, *58*, *65*, *66*, *68*; broadcast, 35, 37, 38, 40, 41, *41*, *42*, 48, 49, *65*, *66*, *68*, 70; paddy, 12, 17, 35, **36**, 36, 37, 39, 40, *40*, 41, *41*, 43, 46, 50, 57, 58, 62, 64, 67, 76, 77; season, 24, *33*, 35, 59, 60; long-stemmed (deepwater), 37, 40; transplanted, 35, 37, 38, 39, 40, 41, 42, 48, 49, 54, 65, *65*, *66*, *68*, 69, 70, 77
Aminul Islam, 25
Aquifers 8, 11, 66
Arabic Script, 6
Aus Paddy, 32, 35, 36, 37, *38*, 38, 40, *40*, 43, 48, 49, 50, 54, *57*, 57, *58*, 58, 60, 62, *65*, *66*, 66, 67, *68*, 69, 70, 77
Awami League, 7

Backswamp depressions, 10, 11, 13, 14, 28, 35, 37, 42, 69
Bagasse, 88
Bamboo, **4**, 24, 50, **51**, **52**, **53**, 84, 88, 91, **91**

Bananas, 50, 52
Bangalees, 1, 3, 4, 5, 6, 7, 73
Barges, **87**, 91
Barrages, 66
Beans, 50, **52**
Benchlands, 9, 10, 49
Bengali, language, 6; literature, 1, 5
Betel nuts, 35
Bhadoi, crops, 32, 39, *65*, *66*, 67, *68*, 69, 70; season, 16, 18 *20*, *21*, 26, 32, *33*, 35, 36, 38, 39, 40, 41, 49, 62, 63, 65, 66, *70*, 91
Bhutto, Mr., 7
Biharis, 5, 73
Birds, 50
Birth rates, 73
Boats, **Frontispiece**, **53**, **82**, 84, **87**, 90, *90*, *91*, 92
Boro, Paddy, 32, **36**, 37, 38, 42, *46*, 46, 48, 49, 50, 54, 56, *57*, 57, *58*, *58*, 59, 60, 62, *63*, *65*, *66*, 67, *68*
Bo tree, 16
Boundaries, alteration of, 4
Braiding, 13
British, education, 5; independence from, 1; rule, 3, 81, 92
Buddhism, 1, 4
Buffalo (*see* Water Buffalo)
'Bustee' Encampments, **82**, 83

Canals, *64*, 67, 69, *70*
Capital accumulation, 56, 95
Capitalists, 95
Carpets, 86
Cattle, *33*, **34**, 35, 49
Cement, 91, 95; cement works, 85
Census of agriculture, 75; of population, 73, *74*, 78

Central government, 6, 7
Chakma (tribe), 54
Chandina rice (IR-532) (*see* H.Y.V. rice)
Channels, 13, **34**, *64*, 66, **67**
Charlands, 11, 13, 14, 39, 40, 41, 71
Chaudhuri, Rahmat Ali, 3
Chickens, **53**, 54
Chillies, 30, 42, 95
Chota Barsat (*see* 'Little Rains')
Cities (*see* Urbanization)
Civil War, 7
Clay soils, 9, 11, 12, 18, 39, 41
Climate, 15–22
Coal, 85
Coasts, 9, 13, 14, 17, 25, *71*, 84
Coconut, 35
Coffee, 54, 55
Colonialism, 6, 7, 95
Communications, 47, 79, 90–4; physical handicaps to, 90–2
Community refuges, 25
Congress (*see* Indian National Congress Party)
Consolidation (*see* Landholdings)
Constructional activity, 10–12
Converts (religious), 5
Cooking oil, 36, 43
Co-operatives, 56, 72
Cotton, 50, **51**, **52**, **55**, 81, 85, 86, 87, 95, 96
Credit (rural), 72
Crocodile, 14
Cropping, distribution, 37–46, *38*, *40*–6, 48, 49, 54; intensity, *65*, *66*, *68*, 75, 76, *76*, 77; regions, seasons (*see* Aman, Bhadoi and Rabi seasons)

Cucumbers, 50
Cultural heritage, 5, 6, 71
Cyclones, 7, 17, *23*, *24*, 23–5, 55, 85

Dao, 50
Death rates, 73
Deer, 14, 50
Deficiency (*see* Diet)
Deltas, 9, 10, 11, 12, 13, 14, 23, 26, 32, 35, 47, 90; deltaic rivers, 10
Democracy, 5, 6, 7
Deposition (*see* Constructional activity)
Depression (cyclonic), 23
Dictatorship, 7
Diet, 29, 35, 43; deficiency, 29, 30, 31, 43, 46
Discrimination, 6
Dissection, 8, **52**
Distributaries, 11, 12, 13, 14
Drainage patterns, 8, 10, 11, 13, 49
Drought, 18, 21, 32, 41, 58
Dry season (*see* Rabi season)
Dry Rabi crops (*see* Rabi)

Earthquake, 10
East India Company, 1
Economy, 1; Development prospects, 95–6; domination, 1, 6, 7, 95; economic imperialism, 3, 84, 87
Elections, 7
Electricity (*see* Power, electric)
Elephants, **52**
El Hamza, 3
Embankments, 12, 14, 25, 28, 41, 69, 70, *70*, *71*; submersible, 28
Engineering, 28, 63, 90
Environment (physical), 8, 62–71
Estuaries, 8, 14, 23, 24
Estuarine islands, 14, 70
Evapo-transpiration, 18

Fats, 30, *31*, 43
Federation (All-India), 3
Fertiliser, 35, 46, 56, 59, **59**, 60, 69, 85, 93
Fish, 30, 31, *31*, 95, 96; fisheries, 46–7, 85, 90; fishing industries, 46–7; fishponds, *30*, 47; freezing, 47

Floods, 7, 10, 13, 17, 24–8, *28*, 32, 35, 36, 37, 39, 41, 42, 43, 48, 49, 56, 58, 60, 69, 76, 77, 90; 49, 56, 58, 60, 69, 76, 77, 90; flood plains, 8, 9, 12, 13, 40, 49; flood protection, 28, 42, 56, 67–70, *69*, *70*; flood refuge, 16, 24, 25
Food grains, **29**, 29, 31, *31*
Foreign aid, 95
Foreign exchange, 6, 7, 95
Fragmentation (*see* Landholding)
Frosts, 16
Fruit, 30, *31*; fruit trees, 35
Fuel, 35

Garjan, 54
Garlic, 42
Gas (*see* Natural Gas)
General elections, 7
Geomorphology, 8, 9–14, *11*
Ginger, 54
Goats, 35, 51
Gourds, 30, 50
Grazing, cattle, 37, 49
'Green revolution', 56, 57, **59**
Groundnuts, 42
Groundwater, 8, 10, 12, 14, 41, 43, 66–7, 79
Gur (*see* Sugar)

Hamza (*see* El Hamza)
Hailstorms, 17
Hardboard, 88
Hardwoods, 54, 88
Hazards (*see* Natural Hazards)
Hegemony (Political), 6
Hides, 90, 95
'High' land agriculture, 35
High-Yielding Variety Rices (H.Y.V.), 16, 26, 28, 39, 41, 56–62, *65*, *66*, *68*, 69, 70; diffusion of, 60, 62; IR-8, 46, 58, 59, 60; IR-20, 60; IR-272 (Mala), 60; IR-442, 60; IR-532 (Chandina), 59
Hill country, 8, 9, 32, 50–5
Hill tribesmen (*see* Tribes)
Hindus, 1, 5, 6, 54; economic domination, 1; landlords, 1, 47, 71
Hoars, 10
Humidity (relative), 16, 46

Hyderabad (Nizam's Dominions), 3
Hydroelectricity development, **53**, 85; potential, 8, 54, 85
Hydrology, 8, 14

Imports, 29, 31, 95–6
India, 1, 71, 73, 85, 86, 93, 95, 96; Army, 5, 7; National Congress Party, 1; Partition, 1, 3, 4, 73, 76, 78, 93; union republic, 1
Independence, 5, 7, 95, 96
Industry, 7, 74, 78, 81, 83, 84, 85–90, **86**, **87**, **88**, **89**
Inland water transport (*see* River)
Innovations, agricultural (*see* Agriculture, innovations)
International Bank for Reconstruction and Development (I.B.R.D.), 7
International Rice Research Institute (I.R.R.I.), 59
Interstream deposits, 12, 13
IQR (interquartile range), 18
IR Rices (*see* High-Yielding Variety Rices)
Irrigation, 7, 13, 38, 39, 42, 49, 54, 56, 58, 59, 60, 63, **63**, 64, 66, 67, **70**, 70, *70*, 76
Islam (*see* Muslims)
Isohyets, 18, *19*, 21

Jack fruit, 35
Jhum cultivation, 8, 32, 50–4, **51**, **52**, *54*
Jinnah, 3, 6
Jute, 6, 7, **10**, 31, 32, 35, 36, 38, 39, **39**, 40 *40*, *41*, 43, 49, *65*, *66*, 68, 85, 87, 88, **89**, 90, 92, 93, 95, 96; mills and textiles, 81, 83, 84, 85, **87**, **88**, **89**; presses, 78, 81, **87**, 96; retting, 36
Jungle, 71, 74

Khesari (pulse), 37, 43
Koran, 6

Lakes, 13, 26, 47, 49, 54
Landforms, 8–14, *11*
Land holdings, consolidation, 72; fragmentation, 65, 71, 72
Landlord, 1, 5, 47
Landparcels (*see* Parcels)
Language problem, 6

Lateritic, 9
Leather, 85, 95; tanning, 90
Levees, **10**, 10, 12, 13, 14, 26, 28, **34**, 35, 43, *64*, 81
Linguistic nations, 1, 5
'Little rains' (Chota Barsat), 18, *20*, 21, *21*, 32, 37, 38, 39, 41, 50
Livestock, 17, 25, 26, *33*, **34**, 35, 37, **51**, **53**, 54
Load (river), 9, 10
Loams, 9, 35, 38, 39
Lodging (rice crop), 59
Lowland agriculture, 35, 35–9, 42

Machinery, 95, *96*
Magh (tribe), **52**, **53**, 54
Maize, 50
Mala rice (IR-272) (*see* H.Y.V. rice)
Malnutrition (*see* Diet deficiency)
Mangoes, 17, 35
Manure (*see* Fertiliser)
Masculinity (*see* Population)
Meanders, 12
Metalwork, 85, *96*
Microclimate, 16
'Middling' land agriculture, 36, 37
Migrants (*see* Population)
Millet, 50, **52**
Milk, *31*, 37
Minorities, 4, 5
Moghul Empire, 1, 5
Moneylender, 1
Monoculture, 12, 41, 42, 48, 49
Monsoon, 15, 37, 69; rains, 12, 36, 37, 41, 90
Mosquitoes, 16
Mro (tribe), **53**, 54, **55**
Muhammad Iqbal, 3
Mujibur Rahman (Sheihk), 6, 7
Mukerjee, Radhakamal, 21
Mulberry, 17
Muslims, 1, 3, 4, *5*, 6, 72, **74**; Muslim league, 1, 3; Muslim nation, 1, 3; percentage, 3, 4, *5*, 5
Muslin, 96
Mustard, 32, 35, 42, 54, *66*

Nagari script, 6
National Assembly (*see* Pakistan National Assembly)
Nationalism, 1, 6
Natural gas, 85, **86**, 96

Natural hazards, 17, 23–8, *23*, *24*, *25*, *28*
Newsprint, 88
Nizam of Hyderabad's dominions, 3
Non-saline tidal delta (*see* Tidal delta)
Nor'westers, 18
Nutrition (*see* Diet)

Oil, 86, 92; power, 85; refineries, 87, 93
Oilseeds, *31*, 32, 36, 42, 43, *44*, 95
Onions, 30, 42
'Openfields', 35

Paddy (*see* Rice)
Pakistan, 54, 73; national assembly, 7; national movement, 3, 7; origins, 1, 3, 5, 6; political collapse, 1; third five-year plan, 87
Palms (coconut), 35
Paper mills, 87, 88, **88**; paperboard, 95
Parcels (of land), 35
Peat, 85
Permeability (soils), 12, 18
Petroleum, 96
Pharmaceuticals, 95
Photo-period, 59, 60
Piedmont, 9, 10, 12, 49
Pigs, 50, **53**, 54
Plains, 9–12
Planning commission, 73
Plantation, 54–5
Plastics, 86
Plywood factories, 90
Polders, 64, 70, 71
Political antecedents, 1–7
Pollution, 47
Population, 73–84; density, 70, 73–7, *74*, *75*; distribution, 6, 78, 79; exchange, 73; increase, 25, 29, 43, 58, 73, *75*, 76, 83, 95; masculinity, 78–9, *79*; migration, 24, 25, 49, 54, 62, 71, 73, 78, 79; pressure, 29, 32, 43, 58, 71, 76, 77; pyramids, 73, *77*, 78
Ports, 84, 93
Portuguese, 81, 84, 93
Potatoes, 30, 42
Power, electric, 9, 64, 66, 81, 84, 85, 96

Protein, 29, 30, *31*, 31, 43, 46
Pucca (jute), 91
Pulses, 30, 31, *31*, 32, 37, 42, 43, *44*, *65*, 90
Pumps, 56, 60, 64, **65**, 70, *70*, **70**, 90; lowlift, 37, 46, 56, 58, **63**, 63, *64*, 66, 72
Punjabis, 3, 5, 6
Purdah (veiling), 73, **74**

Rabi (dry), crops, 32, **34**, 38, *39*, 41, 42, *43*, 43, 49, 54, 56, *65*, *66*, *68*, 69, 70; season, 11, 13, 16, *20*, *21*, *31*, 32, 35, 40, 46, 62, 65, 66, 76, 91
Rahmat Ali, 3
Railways, 81, 83, 84, 90, 91, 92, *92*, 93; broad gauge, 92; metre gauge, 92
Rainfall, 8, 12, *18*, 18, *19*, *20*, *21*, 32, 35, *55*; variability, 18, 21, *22*, 38; rainy season (*see* Bhadoi season)
Rape, 42
Ray, J. K., 4, 6
Refugees, 1, 4, 7, 73, 78, 83
Régimes, River, 26, *27*
Regions, agricultural, 48–55
Religion (*see also* Muslims, Hindus and Buddhism), 1, 3, 4, 5, 6
Retting (of jute), 36
Rice (including paddy) (*see also* Aman, Aus, Boro, H.Y.V. area), production and yields, **10**, 18, 29, 30, 31, **34**, **35**, 47, *48*, 63, 90, 96
Rivers, 9, 8–14, 26–8, 41, 42, 47, 56, 63, 81, 84, 90, 92; cliffs, 13; floodwaters, 8; sediments (*see* Sediments); transport, **Frontispiece**, 81, 83, *90*, 90, 91, **91**, 92, 93, **94**
Road transport, **46**; 92, *92*, **93**
Rubber, 9, 54, 55, 96
Rural Academy, 72
Ryots (peasant farmers), 16

Sal woodland, 12
Salinity, 13, 14, 41, 70–1, 76
Sandy soils, 8, 11, 12, 38
Scripts (*see* Arabic, Nagari)
Sea levels, 9
Sediments (river), 9, 10, 13, 14, 38

Sedimentary rocks, 8
Self-determination, 1, 7
Self-sufficiency (food), 31, *31*, 77
Sensible climate, 16
Separatism, 7, 87
Sesamum, 50
Sex ratios, 78–9
Share cropping, 71, 72
Sheikh Majibur Rahman (*see* Mujibur Rahman)
Shifting cultivation (*see* Jhum)
Ships, 14, 84, 91, **94**
Silk, 17
'Six points' (of Mujibur Rahman), 7
Snakes, 16
Socio-economic environment, 71–2
Softwood, 88
Soil texture, 18, 35, 37, 38, 43, 66, 76, 77
Spices, *31*, 35, 43, 54
Squatters, **82**, 83
Stabilized delta, 13
Standard(s) of living, 7, 73, 83
Steel plant, 87, 93
Storms (*see also* Cyclones), 17, 18
Storm surge, 24, 25, 28
Subsistence farming, 46, 73, 78
Suffrage (universal adult), 7
Sugar, *31*; cane, 32, 35, 42, 43, *45*, **46**, *65*, *66*; factories, mills, processing, 43, *45*, 46, 78, 79, 88; gur, 30, 46
Sunshine records, 16, *17*
Surface water, 62–6

Swales, 13
Swamp reeds, 88
Sweet potatoes, 42
Swidden farming (*see also* Jhum), 32, 50

Tagore, Sir Rabindranath, 15, 16
Tanks, **4**, 12, 25, **34**, 35, 47
Tanning (*see* Leather)
Tea, 91, 93, 95, 96; factories, 54, 78, 85, 88; gardens, 5, 9, 17, 32, 49, 54, **55**, 92
Teak, 9, **52**, 54
Technology, 8, 32, 42, 47, 58, 63, 64, 72, 73, 90
Tectonic instability, 10, 13
Tenchaungya (tribe), **51**, 54
Temperature, 16, *17*, 46, 55
Tenant, 1, 71, 72
Tertiary sediments (*see* Sedimentary rocks)
Textiles (*see* Cotton, Jute)
Tidal, delta, 13, 14, 28, 40, **40**, 41, 43, 48, 49, 64, 67, 70, 75, 76, 77; scour, 14; wave, 24
Tiger, 14
Tipra (tribe), **51**, 54
Tobacco, 32, 35, 36, 42, 54, **89**, 95
Tornadoes, 17
Total cropped area (T.C.A.), 32, *38*, 38, 39, 40, *40*, 41, 41, 42, *42*, *43*, *46*, 62
Tractor ploughing, 37
Trade, foreign, 6, 85–7, 90, 91, 93, 95, 96; transit, 91

Tribes, tribal population, 3, 50, **51**, **52**, 54
Tubewells (*see also* Wells), 60, *64*, 66, 67, **67**, 72, 76
Tumeric, 54

Underdeveloped world, 95
Underfit channels, 10, 12
Urban living, 30, **30**, **80**, **82**, **83**, **88**
Urbanization, 74, 75, 76, 77–84
Urdu, 1, 5, 6

Variability (*see* Rainfall)
Vegetables, 30, *31*, 32, 35, 42, 50, 54, 96
Vitamins, 30

War, 14-day, 5, 7, 29, 78, 91
Water, 8, 41, 66; baskets, 37, **37**; hyacinth, 13, **37**; raising, 37, 56; requirements, 18, 21, 39, 56, 63, 65; scoops, 37, **38**, 47; shovels, 37 (*see also* Groundwater and Tubewells)
Water Buffalo, 37, **46**
Wells, 35, 56, 66
Wet season (*see* Bhadoi season)
Wheat, 29, 32, 42, 43, *45*, *65*, *66*, *68*
Winds (*see also* Cyclones, Storms), 17
Woodland, 12
Wood working, 85, 90
World Bank (*see* I.B.R.D.)

Yahya Kahn (President), 7
Yields, 18, 56, 59, 65, 69

INDEX OF PLACE NAMES, RIVERS AND REGIONS

Afghanistan, 1
Andra Pradesh, 23
Arabian Sea, 23
Arial Khan R., 40, 42
Assam, 2, 4, 8, 26, 32, 81, 84, 91, 92, 93
Atrai-Chalan Bil Depression, 49, 75
Atrai R., 10, 13, 28, 42, 49, 69

Bahadurabad-Ghat, *27, 69*
Bakarganj (Barisal), 79
Baleswar R., *71*, 71
Baluchistan, 2
Balu R., 79
Bandarban, *50*, **53**
Baral R., *69*, 69
Barind (The), 10, 12, 13, 28, 40, 41, 43, 48, *48*, 49, 67, 69, 75
Barisal, 13, 14, 21, 72, 74, 78, 90, 91
Bengal, Bay of Bengal, 8, 9, 14, 16, 23, 47, 84; Bengal Province, 2, 4, 6, 91
Bhairab Bazar, 26, *27*, 28, 49, **93**
Bheramara, 63, *64*, **65**, 85, **89**
Bhola Is., 12, 14, *24*, 70
Bishkhali Channel, 12, *71*, 71
Bogra, 12, 66, *69*, 71, 79, 85
Bombay, 1
Brahmaputra R., 10, 12, 14, **26**, 38, 40, 43, 49; Brahmaputra Left Bank Project, 28, 67, *69*; Brahmaputra–Jamuna R., 13, 26, *27*, 28, 39, 40, 42, 49, 64, 69, 70, 76, 92; Old Brahmaputra, 10, 13, 28, 38, 40, 48, 49
Burhiganga R., **Frontispiece**, 69, *70*, 79, 81
Buriswar Channel, 12
Burma, 8, 32, 78

Calcutta, 2, 4, 16, **17**, *23*, 54, 78, 81, 85, 91, 92, 93, 96
Central Belt (of Lowlands), *48*, 49
Ceylon (*see* Sri Lanka)
Chaggalnaya, **4**
Chaktai Khal R., 84
Chalan Bil, 13, 42, 48
Chalna, 91, 92, 93, **94**
Chandpur, 69, 91
Chandraghona, *50*, **52**, 90; Chandraghona paper mills, 78, 79, **88**, 91
Char Hare, 24
Chhatak, cement factory, 78, 85; paper mill, 88
China, 26
Chittagong, city, 4, 8, 16, *17*, *23*, 47, *50*, 78, 79, 81, 83, 84, 85, **89**, 90, **91**, 91, 92, 93, **94**; coastal plain, 9, 14, 28, *48*, 49, 76, 91; district, 8, 9, 10, 12, 18, 23, 39, 40, 41, 46, 47, 48, 49, 54, 55, 71, 74, 75, 76, 77, 79; hill tracts, 2, 4, 8, 28, 32, 38, 50, **51**, **52**, **53**, *54*, 54, **55**, 71, 74, 79, 85, 88, 96
Comilla, city, 21, 79, 93; district, 12, **34**, 42, 46, 54, 69, 71, 72, 74, 75, 76, 77, 85
Cox's Bazar, 9, 14, 18, *18*, *19*, *21*, 21, *22*, *23*, 25, **34**, 41, *50*, 74

Dacca City, **Frontispiece**, **2**, 2, 6, *18,* *19*, *21*, 21, *22*, *23*, 25, 28, *70*, 77, 78, 79, **80**, 81, *81*, 83, 84, 85, 90, 91, 92, **93**; Dacca–Demrai scheme, *68*, 69; depression, 13; district, 12, **30**, **39**, 46, 49, 69, 74, 75, 76, 77, **83**
Damodar Valley, 96
Delhi, 1

Demra, **36**, *70*, **70**
Dhanmandi suburb (Dacca), 81
Dhaleswari, 13, 28, 42, 49, *69*
Dinajpur City, 16, *17*, *18*, *19*, *21*, 21, *22*; District, 4, 12, 43, 66, **67**, 71, 75, 76, 79
Dohazari, 84

East Bengal, 2, 4, 6, 7, 81 (*see also* E. Pakistan)
East Pakistan, 2, 4, 6, 7, 92, 95 (*see also* E. Bengal)

Farakka Barrage, 64
Faridpur, 5, 13, 49, 71, 74, 76, 77, 79, 85, 92; Faridpur Bil, 13, 28, 42, 49
Fenchuganj (Sylhet), 85, 93
Feni, **4**, **67**
Feni R., 8
Fulchari Ghat, *69*

Gaibandha, *69*
Ganges R., 10, 11, 12, 13, 14, 26, *27*, 28, 40, 41, 43, 49, 92; Ganges–Kobadak Irrigation Scheme, 13, 14, 41, 63, *64*, 64, **65**, 67, 79, 85; Ganges–Plain, 1; Ganges–Padma, 42, 43
Garai R., 64, *64*
Ghaghat R., 10, *69*
Ghorasal (Dacca), 85, 93
Goalundo, 92
Gulshan Model Town (Dacca), 81, *81*
Gumti R., 12, 28, **34**

Hardinge (Railway) Bridge, *27*, *64*, *69,* 92
Haripur, *69*
Hathazari, 84

Hatia Island, 14, 41
Himalaya Foothills, 10, 12
Hoogly R., 64; Hoogly side, 96
Hurasagar R., *69*, 69
Hyderabad (Nizam's Dominions), 2

India, 1, 5, 23, 26, 49, 64, 71, 78,
   81, 86, 91, 93, 96
Indonesia, 78
Iran, 1
Ishurdi, *69*, 88, 92
Islamabad, 7
Iswarganj, 32

Jailpaigura, 16, 92
Jamuna R., 10, 12, 13, *69*, 76, 77,
   91, 92 (*see also* Brahmaputra–
   Jamuna R.)
Jessore, 4, 12, *18*, 19, *21*, 21, *22*,
   71, 79, 92

Kangsa, 49
Kaptai Dam, 8, *50*, 88; Hydel
   project, **53**, 54, 78, 79, 84, 85
Karachi, 7
Karatoya R., 10, *69*, 69
Karnaphuli R., 8, 14, *50*, **53**, 54,
   59, 84, *84*, 85, **91**, 91, **94**
Kasalang Reserve Forest, *50*
Kashmir, 2
Kaunia, *69*, 69
Khulna City, 14, 47, 78, 79, 90, 91,
   92, 93, 96; district, 2, 4, 13, 14,
   41, 64, 74, 79, 85; sundarbans
   (woodlands), 14, 47, 75, 88
Kishoreganj, 62
Kobadak Irrigation Scheme (*see*
   Ganges–Kobadak)
Kumar R., *64*
Kushtia, 12, **35**, 43, **46**, 64, *64*, **65**,
   65, *65*, 46, 71, 76, 79, **89**, 92
Kusiyara R., 91

Lakhya R., 69, *70*, 81, 83
Lalbagh (Dacca), **80**, 83

Madhumati R., 14, 40
Madhupur Tract, 10, 12, 13, 28,
   49, 77, 79
Maiskhal, Is., *50*
Malangipara, *54*
Matamuhari R., 8
Mathabanga R., 12

Meghalaya Plateau, 8
Meghna Basin, 13; depression, 10,
   13, 26, 28, 39, 41, 43, 46, 48,
   49, 62, 75, 85; river, **10**, 10, 12,
   13, 14, 23, 25, 26, *27*, 28, 40,
   42, 48, 49, 69, 75, 79, 91
Mirpur, **46**
Mongla Port, 78, 91, 92, **94**
Moribund delta, 12, 13, 14, 28, 39,
   48, *48*, 49, 64, 75, 91
Murshidabad, 2
Mymensingh District, 10, 13, 28,
   32, 38, 49, 62, 74, 75, 79; town,
   21, 83

Naaf Peninsula, 14
Narayanganj, **29**, *70*, 78, 79, 81,
   83, 85, **89**, 90, 91, 96
Narsingdi, 83
Noakhali District, 12, 14, *24*, 24,
   25, 28, 41, 42, 49, **67**, 69, 71,
   74, 75, 76, 77, 79
Non-Saline Tidal Delta, 49
North Bengal–Brahmaputra Plain,
   48, 49
North Bengal Sandy Alluvial Fan,
   9, 10, 12, 28, 38, 48, 49, 66, 75, 76
Northwest Frontier Province, 2

Old Brahmaputra (*see* Brahmaputra
   R.)
Orissa, 23, 54

Pabna, 21, 42, 74, 76, 77, 79, 88,
   92
Padma R., **10**, 12, 13, 28, 40, 41,
   49, 75, 76, 91
Pakistan, 54, 73, 81, 85, 92, 94, 96;
   national assembly, 7; national
   movement, 7; origins of, 2, 5, 6;
   political collapse, 1; third five-
   year plan (1965–9), 87
Panchbibi, **15**
Patenga Peninsula, 84
Patharghata, *71*, 71
Patuakhali District, 12, 14, *24*, 41,
   71, 75, 76, 79
Pirojpur, 14
Punjab, 1, 2, 4
Purnabhaba R., 10
Pursur R., 14, 92, **94**

Rajshahi, district, 12, 28, 42, 43,
   46, 71, 79; town, 21

Ramgarh, *50*
Ramgati, 41
Ramna Suburb (Dacca), 81, 83
Rangamati, **4**, *50*, **51**, **52**
Rangpur, 12, 21, 43, 66, *69*, 71, 76,
   79
Rawalpindi, 7

Sadarghat, 81, **82**, 83, 84
Saline Tidal Delta, 39, 41, 43, 48,
   48, 49, 64, 70, 75, 76
Sandwip Island, 14, 24, 41, 70
Sangu R., 8
Santahar, *69*
Shahbazpur Channel, 12, 14
Shillong Plateau, 8, 12, 13, 49, 75
Siddirganj, 85
Sind, 2
Sirajganj, *69*, 92
Sitakund Hills, *50*, 84, *84*
Someswari, 49
Sonar Char, 24
South China Sea, 23
Sri Lanka, 78
Stabilised Delta, 28
Sundarbans Forests, 14, 47, 75, 88
Surma R., 91
Sylhet District, 2, 4, 5, 8, 9, 10, 12,
   17, 18, 28, 32, 40, 42, 48, 49,
   54, **55**, 55, 62, 75, 76, 79, 85,
   86, 88; plain, 8; town, **2**, *18*, 18,
   19, *21*, 21, *22*, 49, 92

Tangail (District), 76, 77
Tejgaon, 81
Teknaf, *50*
Tetulia Channel, 12, 14
Thailand, 78
Thakurgaon, *66*, 66, **67**, 67
Tidal Delta, 13, 14, *28*, 28, 40, 49,
   67, 77
Tippera–North Chittagong Plain,
   43, 49, 91
Tippera Surface, 12, 28, 39, 48, 49
Tista Plain, 76
Tista R., 10, 12, 49, 66, 69, *90*
Tripura, 8, 12, 28
Tungi, 83
Turag R., 79

West Bengal, 2, 4, 47, 54, 96
West Pakistan, 4, 5, 6, 7, 54, 95

DATE DUE
